PRAISE
CATHOL

C000088744

"An excellent curriculum of the Christian faith"

"*The Catholic Jesus* is superb. Fr Plant writes beautifully, the book is well written and easy to read. Like any good teacher he not only organises his material well but carefully explains the map of the journey.

"Fr Plant clearly shows the relationship of church and Scripture not simply as a chronological priority but as determining our interpretative method now. He ends with a wonderful meditation on the Eucharist as the place where the church is most itself. Jesus - Scripture - Church - Eucharist. This is an excellent curriculum of the Christian faith.

"Most important of all, however, is the way in which the book fulfils its claim to be describing a catholic Jesus. Jesus is not calling individuals to participate individually in salvation, but individuals are called to become more than themselves by participation in the divine life which is incorporation into the church."

Fr Richard Peers SMMS
Director of Education, Diocese of Liverpool

"The keys to understanding the fundamental mysteries of the Church"

"The Catholic Jesus is an excellent short study of the Christian tradition through the lens of the early Church. Indeed, its effectiveness is found in stressing that the Bible (which the author rightly points out is not an unambiguous notion) cannot be properly understood outside the context of the Church's witness to the reality of Christ and the significance of his person. Furthermore—and in contrast to those who would stress an exclusive focus on scripture (and its inerrancy)—we come to see that it is the Eucharist, as the living presence and source of spiritual grace, that forms the bedrock of religious experience. In this engaging work, Father Thomas Plant gives his readers the keys to understanding the fundamental mysteries of the Church. He does this by tackling—robustly and with great intellectual vigour—the pernicious distortions of modernist reductionism with a view to rehabilitating a faithful defence of an authentic Christian vision. Unreservedly recommended."

Rev John Paraskevopoulos
Hongwanji Buddhist Mission of Australia

THE CATHOLIC JESUS

KNOWING CHRIST THROUGH
THE CHURCH HE FOUNDED

The Catholic Jesus:
Knowing Christ through the Church he founded
Thomas Plant

Dedicated to Aika Maria and Aya Sophia,
who make sense of S. Thomas' dictum:
id quod visum placet.

CONTENTS

INTRODUCTION

Many priests hate preaching on Trinity Sunday. I would go so far as to say they are afraid of it. It is one of the few Sundays of the year, they mutter in distaste, dedicated not to an event in the life of Jesus or his Church, but to a "doctrine."

Ah yes, the "d-word": almost a dirty word, nowadays, and almost invariably prefixed by its alliterative siblings, "dry" and "dogmatic."

Doctrine, you see, is something to be embarrassed about. It's something the Church has made up to dominate the gullible laity and justify its own existence, complicating what are really very simple matters.

And the Trinity is one of the worst of the lot: an act of duplicitous pseudo-mathematics designed to bamboozle people into thinking that a very nice and wise but ultimately just mortal man who lived two thousand years ago is actually God.

So the more-or-less cultured despisers of the Christian religion like to say.

There has been a recent spate of videos on YouTube of very well-meaning and well-versed Muslim evangelists making street conversions of lapsed Christians on the streets. In itself, this is perfectly laudable:

as far as I'm concerned, a practising Muslim working to develop a sense of the one God who is, in the words of the Qur'an, "deeper than the jugular vein," and engaging in prayer, fasting and good works, is a better friend to the Catholic faith than a lukewarm and agnostic "cultural" Christian with no real faith in anything. And yet I find it sad that, at least according to the successes posted on YouTube (I suspect the failed attempts are somewhat less carefully documented!), it seems *so easy* to turn Christians from the very core doctrines of the faith.

The principle target of Islamic proselytism is the Trinity, and in particular the membership of its second person. "How ridiculous," say the evangelists, "to claim that Jesus is God. There is only one God – and that is what Jesus himself taught. He never said that he himself was God. How could that be possible? Jesus even said, 'only God is good!'"

And yes, you will find Jesus saying exactly those words in Mark 10:18. So, one Christian after another, barely knowledgeable of their own sacred scriptures, abandons two thousand year's worth of deep theological reasoning achieved by some of the finest minds known to humanity on the basis of this simplistic reduction.

Of course, how could we not have seen all along how silly it all is?

You don't even have to go outside the Christian fold to find people shuffling their feet in embarrassment around the idea that Jesus is God, or even openly denying it. Take Don Cupitt, a former Anglican priest and now retired fellow of Emmanuel College, Cambridge: he has been arguing since the 80s that Jesus was a liberal wandering rabbi, even a 'secular humanist,' who was later elevated to divine status by the Catholic Church for the preservation of its own interests. He genuinely believes that secular modernity is the apogee of Jesus' teaching, and that we should forget all the religious nonsense of yesteryear. 'Traditional Christianity is modernity's Old Testament,' he proclaims. I must say, I wonder what Jews would make of that easy dismissal of their sacred text.

But Cupitt is nothing new. Long before him, the 19th-century liberal theologian Adolf von Harnack was proudly 'demythologising' Christianity in the search for the 'historic Christ,' who, it emerged from their findings, bore a surprising resemblance to Adolf von Harnack. Who would have known?

But if we really want to find doubts about Jesus' divinity, we can go back further still. As early as AD 110, the Roman governor Pliny was writing to his Emperor, Trajan, that these credulous Christians sang hymns to Jesus as though he were a god, and held tenaciously to the preposterous superstition that he rose from the dead. What humbug!

So no, there is nothing new about controversy over Jesus' divinity. What *is* new is the widespread acceptance even among those who call themselves Christians of this idea: that, if you just scratch the surface, you will find that Jesus was really just a liberal rabbi, only later elevated to a spurious divine status which he never claimed for himself. Its wide acceptance may be new, but actually, the argument itself is very old, and frankly past its sell-by date. In the academic world, it is rejected by all but the most maverick of biblical scholars.

To help you shake off doubts about and doubters of Jesus' divinity, I am going to present historical arguments from *reputable* bible scholars of various shades — not all of whom are even necessarily Christian believers — that Jesus was, as a matter of fact, regarded as divine by the very earliest Christians.

What's more, I am going to argue that Jesus *himself* believed that he was divine, and that really, as C.S. Lewis famously said, one can take only one of two positions on him: either he really was (and is) God and the Son of God, or he was at best deluded, at worst a lying blasphemer.

Of course, the fact that he and his early followers *believed* in his divinity does not mean that it was necessarily so. They might have been wrong (though as a Christian priest, I do not think so). Nonetheless, what is crystal clear is that the middle option of "liberal humanist rabbi" just does not fit the evidence we have of Jesus or of his earliest followers.

Trinity Sunday, it turns out, is not really the celebration of a "doctrine" at all: it is a celebration of *who God is* in the uttermost depths of his nature.

My contention in this short book is to show why.

1. THE HISTORICAL JESUS

So where is the evidence for the claim that Jesus is God?

Well, principally, the New Testament.

"Ah, but—" I hear the dinner-table cynic cry: "surely the New Testament is partisan? Surely it was written by convinced Christian believers?"

And our critical friend would be right. The New Testament is an account of the faith of the early Church, written by and for members of the early Church.

But this is precisely where its value lies. By looking at its component parts in their historic and literary context, we can see quite clearly what the early Christians believed about Jesus, the Church he founded, and we can say something about both his and their approach to the Scripture of the Old Testament. I do not think for a moment that one can look behind the Church and her Scriptures to find a pristine and objective record of the historical Jesus.

But, if we look at the interplay between the three — Jesus, the Church and the Bible — as though we are crossing our eyes at one of those Magic Eye pictures from the 1990s, like the three-dimensional dolphins and deer from those books, a clearer image of the belief of our earliest forebears in the faith will emerge.

Our first task, if we are going to look at the earliest Christian sources, is to work out what they are. I wonder, if I gave you a list of books in the New Testament, whether you could put them in roughly chronological order of when they were written?

A hint: it's not the order that they are printed in in modern Bibles: that is, first the gospels, then Acts, the letters (or 'epistles') and finally the Revelation (or Apocalypse) of St John. So, before you move on, you may like to look at the contents of the New Testament section of your own copy of the Bible, and consider roughly what order you think it was written in. Which do you think was written first?

Here is the New Testament in roughly and somewhat debatable chronological order, interspersed in italics with contemporary but non-biblical Christian texts and one or two significant events:

c.6BC	Birth of Christ
c.AD30	Crucifixion
51 – 53	Letters from Paul to communities
51	1&2 Thessalonians (on the coming of Christ)
56-58	1&2 Corinthians, Galatians, Philippians, Romans (Paul on righteousness and justification)

61-63	Colossians, Ephesians (probably not Paul), Philemon (from prison in Rome: on the cosmic Christ)
[?60-150	?Paul or a disciple: Titus, 1 & 2 Timothy (on church organization and order)]
64	1 Peter (from Rome to Jewish Christi an diaspora on Exodus and baptism)
?67	Hebrews (not by Paul)
?50-120	Didache - 'Teachings of the Apostles'
?50-140	Gospel of Thomas
70	Romans destroyed Temple
c.70	Gospel of Mark
80-90	Luke and Acts (written by the same person)
80-90	Matthew
c.80-120	Jude (against false teachings)
80-120	Epistle of "Barnabas" on abrogation of Old Law
80-100	1 Clement: Bishop of Rome to the Church of Corinth, refers to deacons and bishops
90-95	Revelation of St John
95 - 120	Johannine writings: John and 1 John (3 John and 2 John probably a little earlier)
c. 100	2 "Peter" (beware of false teachings; inspiration of Scripture, 1.20-21)
105-115	St Ignatius of Antioch: on episcopacy

First, note that the Gospels, the only direct accounts of Jesus' life and teachings, were written between forty and ninety years after he had died.

The earliest Christian sources are the letters of St Paul. Interesting to note that they focus on the mission to gentiles, that is, the non-Jews whom Paul calls "Greeks." From the earliest of these, the letters to the Thessalonian church, it seems that the earliest thing Christians were interested in was the imminent second coming of Christ.

Perhaps because this started to look like it was going to take longer than he had expected, Paul then started pondering (in 1 & 2 Corinthians, Galatians, Philippians, Romans) how exactly one was 'made righteous' or justified in Christ, and the relation between this new Covenant with God and the old one, enshrined in the Jewish Law of the Torah.

Writing from prison in Rome, Paul's next epistles (Colossians, Ephesians, Philemon) are concerned with the cosmic nature of Christ and his historical significance in the salvation of the world.

The next set of letters possibly written by Paul, but more likely by some of his disciples (Titus, 1&2 Timothy), focus on putting right some flaws in church organization. Yes, that's right: Christians were writing about *church order* before the completion of the gospels, and this does matter, for reasons we will come to later.

After Paul's mostly gentile-focused letters from prison, we have a couple written with Jewish communities in mind: one attributed to Peter, and another (almost certainly falsely) to Paul, the Letter to the

Hebrews. The next Christian writing may well have been the anonymous *Didache* or 'Teaching of the Twelve Apostles,' which focuses particularly on proper order at the Eucharist and gives detailed accounts of two forms or perhaps two aspects of the ritual meal. So, once again, note: writings about the Church and the Eucharist *predate* the completion of the gospel biographies of Jesus. This tells us something about the nature of early Christian priorities.

Only after this, around AD 70, is the first account of Jesus' life, death and resurrection set down for posterity in the terse Gospel according to St Mark, Jesus' shortest biography, written in the most straightforward, everyday Greek – which was the *lingua franca* of the ancient Middle East in the same way as English is the *lingua franca* of much of the world today.

Luke and the Acts of the Apostles, which were written by the same author, probably came next. Many scholars maintain that this account was written by a gentile for gentiles, following Luke's traditional identity as a Greek medical doctor, in far more flowing and self-consciously classical Greek— though Luke's knowledge of Judaism makes this claim somewhat contentious, and nowadays the hard line between ancient 'Jew' and 'Greek' is increasingly regarded as a fiction. The Jews had lived under Greek and then Roman rule for centuries, and their literary and ruling classes were, in modern parlance, very much integrated with the Greco-Roman milieu in which they lived. At any rate, the author wrote both his account of the Gospel — the 'Good News' or biography of Jesus — and in Acts, the most complete account of the life of the Early Church.

Around the same time, Matthew also appears, painting a picture of Jesus as a teacher and lawgiver, more closely following the pattern of a Jewish rabbi, and probably with more of a Jewish audience in mind. It is likely that both Matthew and Luke had access to Mark and also to another lost account, or perhaps to shared notes in circulation at the time.

Before the last gospel is written, we have the epistle written by someone called Jude, possibly the 'brother' of Jesus, whatever that means (among the ancient Jews, the word could indicate any member of the extended family). This is sent out to warn against false teachers at the *agape* 'love feasts' who 'deny' our Lord Jesus Christ.

Around the same time, now outside the biblical canon, Bishop Clement of Rome writes to upbraid the faithful in Corinth who do not respect their own bishops, priests and deacons. Again, note that before the New Testament is even complete, we have references here from an early Christian leader to the nascent orders or the Church, including bishops, priests and deacons.

Clement's use of the scripture warns us against anachronistic ideas about the Bible. He cites what we now call "Scripture," works which are now in the Bible, especially the Letter to the Hebrews, and includes allusions to some of Paul's letters, Acts, James and 1 Peter. But! - *he does not call them scripture at all:* salient for us as we think about what Jesus' earliest followers would think of our concept of "the Bible."

There is no evidence to suggest that St Paul and the other New Testament writers thought that they were writing scripture themselves, nor that contemporary Christians regarded their writings as such. Jesus and his followers had no bibles, and for them, Scripture meant what we call the Old Testament, which was not by and large carried around and read in private, but publicly read or sung as part of the ritual of their solemn religious gatherings.

Only after all this was the body of works known as the 'Johannine corpus' formed: that is, the works attributed to St John and most likely written down from his collected notes and sayings by a group of his closest followers. John's works are the most mystical-seeming of the New Testament, and arguably the most explicit in proclaiming Jesus as divine.

So, the clearest affirmations of Jesus as God come only as late as seventy years after he was crucified. What is more, even the very first writings about Jesus were written by St Paul some twenty years after the death of a man he never actually met in the flesh, and that is a delay long enough for some serious distortion to take place. You can see how critics might see Christ's divinization as a gradual process, straying ever more away from the reality of the simple historical rabbi as time presses on. Their idea is that John's Jesus is very different from Paul's Jesus, and for that matter, John's church is very different from Paul's church. Both got 'higher,' as it were, as time went on, in tandem with the other. As the Church's importance swelled, they say, so did her claims about Jesus.

So, the evidence of the New Testament seems stacked against us. But is St Paul's view of Jesus really that distant from the life of the man himself? And is it really so different from St John's?

Let us take the first contention first: the fact that St Paul, the earliest Christian writer, never met Jesus and wrote two decades after his death. Our earliest Christian records are no closer than 20 years to actual, face-to-face contact with Jesus, and what's more, they are written by someone who acknowledges quite openly that he never met Jesus in his mortal lifetime. So, are we left with an unbridgeable gap between the Jesus of history and the Christ of the Church, or the "Good Man Jesus and the Scoundrel Christ," as the influential children's author Philip Pullman puts it?

Next chapter, let's ask St Paul.

2. THE THESSALONIANS' JESUS

My argument against the assumption that Jesus was gradually exaggerated by the Church so far might not look very convincing.

Just to run through the chronology again, there was a gap of twenty years between Jesus' death on the Cross and the first Christian writings by St Paul, who never actually met Jesus in his lifetime anyway. The first Gospel, attributed to St Mark, was not written for another twenty years, and the last Gospel, written by St John and his followers was not around until the end of the century. And that is where the claims for Jesus' divinity, the Word made Flesh, are most obvious.

So far, then, it does look like the concept of Jesus as God was a gradual development over a good seventy years. Perhaps he *was* just a liberal rabbi who ended up used by a power-hungry Church to further its own prospects.

But the 'liberal rabbi' argument will hold only if we find that Paul's view of Jesus really is all that different from John's, or that Paul invented a version of Jesus which was different from the real person.

So first, a bit about Paul. A native of the cosmopolitan city of Tarsus on the South coast of what is now Turkey, Paul was a Greek-speaking Jew, and a Pharisee at that, born within ten years of Jesus. He would have grown up in a multi-racial and -cultural environment, most likely speaking Aramaic and Latin as well as his native Greek. Pharisees often faced Jesus' scorn, although he had more in common with them than with the rival Saduccee sect— against the view of the Saduccees, at least the Pharisees (like modern Muslims) agreed with Jesus that there would be a resurrection.

Nonetheless, Pharisees were no friends of the early Church. The Acts of the Apostles tells us that Paul was a tent-maker by trade, and Paul himself tells us he was a zealous persecutor of the first Christians. Acts also tells us (three times!) of his famous 'conversion' on the road to Damascus, which can be reliably dated from his own account in the Epistle to the Galatians to somewhere between AD 32 and 34 – that is, only two or three years after Jesus' death.

In his own writing, Paul does not relate the famous story of how he saw a vision and fell down, blinded by the sight of the Risen Lord – the full version is found only in Acts – but what he does write is, God 'revealed his son to me' (Galatians 1.16). Whatever that revelation was, it was profound enough to make him want to join the Christian movement and, by the end of the 30s, to start his mission to gentiles (non-Jews) in Antioch. He wrote his first letter to the Thessalonians some sixteen to eighteen years later, the earliest extant Christian writing, but importantly, he had already been a Christian for many years before writing it.

This means that those who want to maintain that Paul instigated a dramatic makeover of Jesus from wandering Rabbi to universal saviour need to explain how this happened in the space of less than two decades. They are also going to have to tell us how Paul managed to change the minds of so many Jewish Christians, most of the Apostles among them, in the time between then and Jesus' death.

It is tempting to think that because we have a lack of written sources between Jesus' death and the first of Paul's letters, nothing much happened then. But on reflection, that simply cannot be true. Paul did not start a movement; he joined one which already existed, and when he writes his first letters, he does so as a man in his early fifties with almost two decades' experience in the mission field within communities that he has been a part of since his mid-thirties.

It is worth having a look at what Paul, this experienced missionary, says about Jesus in these earliest letters, and also the way he says it.

Take our earliest text, St Paul's First Epistle to the Thessalonians. You will find that he is not writing alone, but with his companions Silvanus and Timothy, and notably he does so not just in 'God the Father' but, in the same breath, also in 'the Lord Jesus Christ':

"Paul, Silvanus, and Timothy, to the Church of the Thessalonians *in God the Father and the Lord Jesus Christ*: Grace to you and peace." (1 Thessalonians 1.1)

Thessalonica was the second city in Europe after Philippi (about 95 miles away) where Paul preached the gospel, according to Luke in Acts 17. It still exists, as modern day Salonica. There, Paul went to the synagogue, where he found both Jews and the so-called "God-fearing gentiles," those Greeks who were impressed by Jewish monotheism as compared with the devotions and sacrifices of their native pagan religions. This is how Acts 17.1-4 puts it:

> "Now when they had passed through Amphipolis and Apollonia, they came to Thessalonica, where there was a synagogue of the Jews. And Paul went in, as was his custom, and for three weeks he argued with them from the scriptures, explaining and proving that it was necessary for the Christ to suffer and to rise from the dead, and saying, 'This Jesus, whom I proclaim to you, is the Christ.' And some of them were persuaded, and joined Paul and Silas; as did a great many of the devout Greeks and not a few of the leading women."

According to Luke, then, Paul stayed there for a few weeks and, by arguing from the Jewish scriptures (bearing in mind that there were no New Testament scriptures yet) he persuaded several Jews and pagans to join his cause.

If we compare this description in Acts with Paul's own earlier letters, though, we run into some difficulties. First, it seems Paul stayed rather longer in Thessalonica than just a few weeks:

> "For you remember our labour and toil, brethren; we worked night and day, that we might not burden any of you, while we preached to you the gospel of God." (1 Thessalonians 2.9)

Paul and his colleagues "worked night and day" to sustain themselves, presumably to pay for food and shelter, so that they could preach "the gospel of

God," which implies that they were not just there in the short term. The money they brought with them did not cover their expenses. By the time he writes his letter, he has also managed to set up an organisation with some hierarchy:

> "But we beseech you, brethren, to respect those who labor among you and are over you in the Lord and admonish you, and to esteem them very highly in love because of their work." (1 Thessalonians 5.12-13)

It would take some time to establish even a rudimentary hierarchy, setting some 'over' others to admonish them and be esteemed or revered.

Also, Paul was there long enough that some members of the community had even died by the time he writes:

> "But we would not have you ignorant, brethren, concerning those who are asleep, that you may not grieve as others do who have no hope." (1 Thessalonians 4.13)

Rather more than three weeks must surely have passed between the establishment of the Christian church in Thessalonica and writing of the letters to them. The early Church maintained that Paul wrote the letter very soon after leaving Thessalonica, from Athens, but modern scholars more commonly believe that it was written from Corinth, the city he stopped in after Athens. We do not need to get into the arguments here, because either way, these point to a date of around AD 51, during the consulship of Gallio as mentioned in Acts 18.12. The internal evidence of 1 Thessalonians suggests that Paul had left Thessalonica only a year or two before writing: so, his mission there was in the late 40s. We have in these letters, then, evidence of a young Christian community established in a fairly short time by a group of experienced Christians led by Paul.

So, what Paul says to the Thessalonian church about Jesus will give us an idea of what some of the earliest Christians believed. We have already seen how Paul places Jesus with God the Father right in the opening sentence of the letter ("to the Church of the Thessalonians in God the Father and the Lord Jesus Christ")— but there is far more to glean from 1 Thessalonians than just that: namely, that *Jesus is God's Son who has died and risen, and will come again to save by granting eternal life to the faithful.*

First, Paul states without any apparent controversy that *Jesus has died and risen*:

> "We believe that Jesus died and rose again" (1 Thessalonians 4.14).

If this were a controversial statement, he would have needed to argue it, but clearly the Christians he is writing to treat it as a matter of fact. So, we can say that the very first Christians of which we have any record, those formed within the first twenty years of Jesus' death, believed in his Resurrection. Let this be our first enticement away from the belief that he was just some liberal rabbi.

Second, they seem to accept without argument that *Jesus is God's Son and will come again to raise the faithful dead*. Paul exhorts them:

> "…to wait for his Son from heaven, whom he raised from the dead, Jesus who delivers us from the wrath to come" (1 Thessalonians 1.10).

How, we might justifiably ask, would the early Christians think that Jesus could rescue them from judgment if he were just a dead rabbi?

Quite clearly, their hope was in the second coming or "Advent" of Christ:

"For what is our hope or joy or crown of boasting before our Lord Jesus at his coming?" (1 Thessalonians 2.19).

At that point, says Paul,

"the Lord himself will descend from heaven with a cry of command, with the archangel's call, and with the sound of the trumpet of God. And the dead in Christ will rise first" (1 Thessalonians 4.16).

Further, Jesus gives the early Christians not just a future hope for resurrection, but has power to change their lives in the here-and-now through the divine gift of love:

"May the Lord make you increase and abound in love to one another and to all men, as we do to you, so that he may establish your hearts unblamable in holiness before our God and Father, at the coming of our Lord Jesus with all his saints." (1 Thessalonians 3.12-13)

Jesus is taking prime place in the economy of salvation. While none of this definitively indicates that Paul is actively identifying him with God, it certainly puts him much closer to God than a dead rabbi, however good and holy.

Third, the early Christians accept that *Jesus is saviour*, and is fundamental to God's purposes for them. Paul writes that:

"God has not destined us for wrath, but to obtain salvation through our Lord Jesus Christ, who died for us so that whether we wake or sleep we might live with him" (1 Thessalonians 5.9).

Right here, in the earliest Christian writing, we see the Christian belief that Jesus' death and resurrection was *for them* and, in some way, gave them *eternal life*.

It is also worth observing exactly *how* St Paul writes all of these things about Jesus. He makes no argument. There is no sense that he is trying to persuade the Thessalonians. This is not presented to its recipients as a controversial letter. Paul is setting down quite simply what he understands his fellow Christians already believe. With this belief, he wants them to "comfort one another" (1 Thessalonians 4.18) so that they can "stand fast in the Lord"(1 Thessalonians 3.8) in time of persecution (1 Thessalonians 1.6, 2.14).

The final point to make about this letter is what Paul does not say, for what is unsaid speaks volumes - and indicates more clearly the nature of its intended recipients. It tells us what the Thessalonians were like.

At no point in 1 Thessalonians does Paul quote Scripture— unlike in so many of his later letters. There is no evidence that this particular community of earliest Christians shared the "Bible-believing" priority of many of their modern successors today.

At no point in this letter does Paul refer to Jesus as the Jewish Messiah. This may well have simply been assumed, but at any rate, it did not seem to be a priority for the Thessalonians.

At no point in this letter does Paul refer to the Jewish faith he would share with the recipients of the letter if they were in fact fellow Jews: on the contrary, the only reference he makes to Jews in the letter is in 1 Thessalonians 2.14, and it is not exactly a positive one.

From this, to whom should we surmise Paul is writing? Presumably, to gentile converts. This is why scriptural quotes would have meant little to them at this stage, the notion of the Messiah would have been alien, and their main experience so far of Jews had been as persecutors— as indeed St Paul himself had once been. This is not to say at all that 1 Thessalonians is an anti-Jewish letter, only that St Paul is writing on this occasion with a gentile audience in mind.

Let's put this all together. 1 Thessalonians, the earliest written testimony we have of Christian faith, reveals to us a missionary Church that has spread to Macedonia and Achaia (1 Thessalonians 1.8). It has a rudimentary hierarchy, and is part of a wider network of churches (2 Thessalonians 1.4). Notably, there is no sign here that what Paul writes departs in any way from the teaching of these other churches, with which he seems to be on amicable terms.

The letter appears to have been written to a predominantly gentile church, teaching the gospel of Jesus Christ in understandable terms, yet in no way appearing to provoke any controversy with Jewish believers. It does not talk about Jesus the Rabbi, Jesus the Messiah (except insofar it calls him 'Christ,' which is the Greek word for Messiah, a Hebrew word meaning 'anointed'), even Jesus the Jew. Rather, it talks about Jesus the Saviour, Jesus the Son of God, Jesus resurrected by the Father, Jesus who will come again to awaken the faithful dead and so gives hope to the living. Even though these assertions might make only limited sense outside of Jesus' Jewish context, Paul does not see fit to emphasise it here.

You would think that if the earliest Christians actually viewed Jesus as just a great rabbi, then this earliest Christian letter would be very controversial. In reprisal, we would expect the next generation of Jewish writers, such as Mark and Matthew and Peter, to raise very serious objections. We do know from the various letters that there were arguments between Paul and the Peter. But once Barnabas has introduced Paul to the Apostles, never is he excluded or condemned.

On the contrary, as we will see, Paul's testimony is amplified and condoned in the gospels and the other letters.

3. THE PRE-PAULINE JESUS

I fear I may have slightly misled you when I said that the letters to the Thessalonians are the earliest written Christian testimony we have.

These are, few doubt, the earliest *complete* writings we have. But within the letter to the Philippians, written about five years later, many believe there is an older passage still, called by scholars a 'Christological hymn:'

> "Have this mind among yourselves, which is yours in Christ Jesus, who, though he was in the form of God, did not count equality with God a thing to be grasped, but emptied himself, taking the form of a servant, being born in the likeness of men. And being found in human form he humbled himself and became obedient unto death, even death on a cross. Therefore God has highly exalted him and bestowed on him the Name which is above every name, that at the name of Jesus every knee should bow, in heaven and on earth and under the earth, and every tongue confess that Jesus Christ is Lord, to the glory of God the Father." (Philippians 2.5-11)

This 'hymn' does fit into the context of the letter to the Philippians, written to the 'saints, bishops and deacons' there to encourage them to stand firm in the faith while Paul himself was imprisoned in Rome. Yet many scholars believe that its poetic qualities echo older Hebrew and Aramaic metres, that the language used is unusual for Paul, and that the order of salvation presented here differs from how Paul presents it in most of his other writings. There are some scholars who point to similar examples elsewhere in Paul, but it does seem sufficiently different from most of his writing to support the supposition that it is an older, possibly even Semitic, hymn which Paul is reciting from memory.

This hymn represents the earliest complete statement of "Christology"— the doctrine of the person of Christ. Even if we take the later date, we are looking at a hymn of praise about Jesus apparently taken as read and considered uncontroversial among believers only thirty years at most after Jesus' death; but we may well be looking at something far earlier than that.

That unusual phrase "in Christ Jesus" which we first met in 1 Thessalonians comes back at the beginning of the Christological hymn. Paul uses it pretty consistently to describe his fellow faithful.

But in other respects, this passage is quite different from that earlier letter. For a start, where the letters to the Thessalonians are mostly devoid of content drawn obviously from Jewish tradition, this 'hymn' is replete with scriptural references. And yet each reference is paradoxically opposed with an image that would shock the more conservative Jew of the time.

For a start, what might "the form of a servant" make the Jewish listener think of? Taken with Jesus' humbling and obedience to death on the Cross proclaimed here, it would call attention immediately back to the prophet Isaiah's image of the "Suffering Servant" prophesied there:

"He was despised and rejected by men; a man of sorrows, and acquainted with grief; and as one from whom men hide their faces he was despised, and we esteemed him not. Surely he has borne our griefs and carried our sorrows; yet we esteemed him stricken, smitten by God, and afflicted. But he was wounded for our transgressions, he was bruised for our iniquities; upon him was the chastisement that made us whole, and with his stripes we are healed. … Yet it was the will of the Lord to bruise him; he has put him to grief; when he makes himself an offering for sin, he shall see his offspring, he shall prolong his days … by [the Lord's] knowledge shall the righteous one, my servant, make many to be accounted righteous; and he shall bear their iniquities." (Isaiah 53)

We should be aware at this point that modern Jewish scholars do not regard the Isaiah text as a prophecy of the coming Messiah, the Greek word for which is "Christ." However, Margaret Barker in her various works on Temple Mysticism presents evidence that *in Jesus' time*, Jewish tradition did treat it in this way, and moreover as prophecy of an eternal high priest who would offer sacrifice in the temple of heaven.

But that is not the cause for scandal I wish to draw our attention to here. Rather, it is in the parallel phrase to the 'form of a servant' a couple of lines earlier: the hymn claims that Jesus was 'in the form of God,' and even 'equal to God.'

Within the Jewish scriptures, which Christians call the Old Testament, the Jewish leaders of Jesus' time gave greater priority to the law book of Deuteronomy than to what is known as the "wisdom literature." Most were strictly monotheistic. There is evidence that some contemporary Jewish sects were more open to the intermediary work of angels and blurred the boundary between God and creation. However, in mainstream Judaism – or at least, among those who held religious and political power at the time – to claim that Jesus, a man, was in the "form of God" and "equal to God" was blasphemy: and not some later invention of the Church, but very early Christian blasphemy, as we can see from this hymn in the letter to the Philippians.

Lest we are in any further doubt, the Christological hymn in Philippians speaks of God granting Jesus "the Name above every name." This refers to what the Hebrew scriptures refer to as the *Shem ha Shem*, 'name of names,' the transcendent and mysterious 'name' of God Himself. This is so sacred that while it can be *written* by the four letters YHWH — which would sound something like "Yachveh" — when the scriptures are read in Jewish worship, the Name is never, ever spoken out loud. Instead of pronouncing YHWH, pious Jews supply a different word: *Adonai*, meaning 'Lord.' It is as though in English, every time you see the word 'God' written, you *say* 'Lord' instead. So when the hymn concludes that 'every tongue' should profess Jesus to be this 'Lord,' *kyrios* in Greek, it is making a powerful statement.

More powerful still, while the *tongue is confessing* that Jesus is Lord, that Jewish euphemism for God's sacred name, the *knee should also be bending*. For a mainstream Jew in Jesus' day, this bending of the knee is homage which should be given to God alone — and the hymn goes even further, claiming that not only the knees of mortals, but *every knee in heaven* should bend to Jesus, too.

That line about every tongue confessing God is plucked pretty much verbatim from the Greek version of the Old Testament which Paul and his fellow Greek-speaking Jews would have known. Most Jews of the day did not actually speak Hebrew, but relied on a Greek translation called the Septuagint (meaning "seventy" in Greek, because it was supposedly translated by seventy scholars, and so is often referred to in writing by the Roman numerals LXX).

What many people do not realise is that even though it the Septuagint is a translation, in many ways it is more reliable than the Hebrew Old Testaments we have now: because recent manuscript evidence (such as scrolls famously discovered at Qumran) shows that the Hebrew texts were doctored by rabbis in the early Christian era to remove anything which might support Christian belief. For those interested in finding out more, Margaret Barker's *Temple Theology: An Introduction* provides a very readable summary of this process.

Returning to the connection of the Septuagint with the Christological hymn, in this Greek version of

Isaiah 45.23, God himself says, "to me every knee shall bow, every tongue shall swear." So, God is speaking the *very words* which the Christological hymn will later use to refer to Christ— emphasising that all heaven and earth should pay Jesus the worship owed to God alone.

The controversial identification of Jesus with God becomes even more apparent when we look at what God had said in the same passage of Isaiah almost immediately before:

> "Turn to me and be saved, all the ends of the earth! For I am God, and there is *no other*" (LXX: Isaiah 45.22).

Yet the early Christological hymn of the Epistle to the Philippians does seem to be suggesting "another"— unless, that is, it is saying that Jesus and God are one and the same.

So, to recap: according to this ancient hymn, Jesus is in the form of God, he empties himself of divine qualities to take the form of the Suffering Servant, is given the sacred, unspeakable name of God and receives worship due to God alone.

If Jesus is not God, then this very early hymn of Christian belief is utterly idolatrous. That, no doubt, is what both the Romans and Jews who persecuted the earliest Christians thought.

The evidence we have seen so far suggests that the earliest Christians, whether the Thessalonians, or the community that formed Paul in his first twenty years of ministry, who perhaps sung the Christological hymn we have just studied, believed that Jesus was a divinely sent saviour, Son of God and equal to God, fit to be worshipped as God Himself.

But that still leaves us with a question. Did Jesus think the same himself? Or is there still, perhaps, scope for the idea that even in such a short time, even in the twenty years between his death and the first of Paul's letters, the burgeoning Christian Church misrepresented him?

To answer this, we are going to have to get as close as we can to what Jesus said about himself—which takes us from the epistles to the gospels.

4. THE JESUS OF THE GOSPELS

In the first chapter, we sketched out what I think is nowadays the predominant popular portrait of Jesus as a dangerously liberal or radical rabbi which evolved into the idea that he was God much later, all for the convenience of the Church.

We promptly scribbled a moustache and pair of comedy glasses onto that portrait, as it were, when we put the New Testament into chronological order and saw that such an evolutionary model really does not apply.

Then, in the previous two chapters, I tried to score that picture out altogether by showing that the very earliest Christian testimony, both in Paul's earliest letters and in the apparently pre-Pauline Christological hymn of Philippians 2.5-11, already treated Jesus as universal saviour and put him in the place properly reserved for God.

From what we have seen, the actual teachings of Jesus as a rabbi did not seem to be the most important thing to the earliest Christians. But just in case a bit of the long-haired secular humanist of the 20th century Jesus is still smiling through my crayon marks,

I now want to blot it out conclusively by reference, as far as possible, to Jesus himself. I want to see how he saw himself.

You may have seen Monty Python's *the Life of Brian*, or at least heard of it. I have just shown what the earliest Christian testimony says about Jesus. But this does not in itself mean that the Monty Python version of his story is necessarily wrong. It could still be that Jesus himself was just an ordinary chap, a "Brian" whom other people kept calling the Messiah, despite his earnest protestations to the contrary.

The place to find out whether this is so would be the gospels, the biographies of Jesus, those four accounts of Jesus' life and teachings which come at the beginning of modern copies of the New Testament.

But here we have a problem.

We saw in Chapter 1 that even the first of the Gospels, Mark, was written around AD 70, Matthew and the Luke-Acts omnibus some ten to twenty years later, and John as late as AD 100, some seventy years after Jesus' death. This surely gave its authors quite some scope for elaboration, especially since Jesus was not around (in the flesh, at least) to contradict them. How do we know they didn't just make it all up?

Detractors who want to dismiss the gospel accounts often point out the historical inconsistencies between them, especially between John and the three so-called 'synoptics' (a Greek word meaning those who 'share the same view'). How, for example, could the Last Supper have taken place on two different days? Or what about the differences between accounts of Jesus' precise words, or of the miracles?

31

Surely these discrepancies mean that none of the stories is trustworthy.

But think about it. If the Church were really engaged in some great cover-up and wanted to con the world into believing what it said about Jesus, it has had plenty of opportunity to iron out all of these inconsistencies. Very few of our Greek manuscripts date from before the tenth century, so the Church was not short of time to do so some editing. The fact remains that she has not done so.

could have edited out

Editing out the inconsistencies has never been considered necessary: not because the Church has believed that the Bible is 'verbally inerrant,' a literal historical account of events with no human error or inconsistency— that is a very modern notion; but rather, because the Gospel accounts are believed to have been collated from the testimony of *eye witnesses.*

Read?

Imagine a crime scene. As any policeman will tell you, ask any three witnesses about the details of the crime they've just seen, and you'll get three different accounts. Events will be in a slightly different order. You may even get quite different descriptions of the culprit.

Ask those three people some years after the event, and the stories will diverge even more. It's not because they are lying, but because they remember differently. And that, we should be careful to remember, is how history is made, including modern media reports. The historian or the reporter can try to be as objective as possible, but will never get down to the 'plain facts,' even if he was there and saw it with his own eyes: because *even the evidence of our eyes is filtered by our minds*, in whatever way our minds have been pre-conditioned to perceive events. So, if all the biblical eye witnesses had said exactly the same thing, it simply would not ring true. The reader would smell a rat. It is not so strange after all, then, that our gospel accounts should differ, and in fact this positively attests to a *lack* of meddling by the Church.

While we are at it, let's put the time lapse between the Crucifixion and the writing of the Gospels into perspective.

There has long been an assumption among historians that the transmission of the gospel narratives was delivered by an oral tradition stretching back over a generation or two. But bear in mind that even if Mark was written as late as AD 70, Paul and Peter had died only three years ago: not so long after all. Certainly, not long enough to forget everything they had said, unless we are to accuse the evangelists of amnesia as well as mendacity. It would also make sense if it were the death of these first eye-witnesses which prompted the gospel writers to write their memoirs down for posterity.

The Gospels

Professor Richard Bauckham puts forward a compelling case in his 2006 book *Jesus and the Eyewitnesses*. Luke, he notes, uniquely begins his Gospel with an explicit appeal to eyewitness testimony:

> "Inasmuch as many have undertaken to compile a narrative of the things which have been accomplished among us, just as they were delivered to us by those who from the beginning were eyewitnesses and ministers of the word, it seemed good to me also, having

followed all things closely for some time past, to write an orderly account for you, most excellent Theophilus, that you may know the truth concerning the things of which you have been informed." (Luke 1:1-4)

Note that Luke here refers to previous similar attempts at compiling eyewitness accounts, and names the eyewitness as those ministers or "servants" of the Word who were with Jesus "from the beginning." Bauckham argues that this refers to the Twelve Apostles.

This sort of reference to eyewitnesses is not restricted to the Bible. It is entirely typical of contemporary pagan historiography, and this does fit in with the traditional portrayal of Luke as a learned gentile— his Greek is regarded as the best in the New Testament canon.

And yet there is something quite atypical, and unexpected, about the witnesses Luke calls upon. First, he does seem to draw considerably from Mark's gospel— nothing unusual about that. Bauckham argues convincingly that the Gospel of Mark is based primarily on Peter's first-hand testimony. But Luke, he says, augments this "Petrine" perspective with further eyewitness testimony of Jesus' *women disciples*: that is, the witness of a section of people whose testimony would be considered invalid in Jewish courts and would not be taken seriously by the intelligentsia of the occupying Roman Empire.

Is Luke, then, a feminist Gospel? The notion is ahistorical and would not have crossed Luke's mind, but it may well be worth at least bearing the question in ours the next time we read or hear him. If Bauckham is right, it at least points towards the Early Church as a society which placed greater trust in women than most of its contemporary society. For our purposes, there is every reason to suppose that many of these women would have still been alive when Luke's gospel was written, that they would have been able to object to any distortions, and that their voices would have been heard.

The question of Matthew's sources, Bauckham argues, is more complicated, drawn from a broader range of witnesses without that clear focus on Peter's testimony which characterizes Mark. Early in the second century, a follower of John called Papias wrote about the formation of the gospels. According to Papias, Matthew himself was an eyewitness and put various "logia," or recorded sayings of Jesus, together in a literary order in his native language of Aramaic, the closest spoken relation to the written biblical language of Hebrew (there is a parallel here in early collation of the *hadith*, or sayings, of Muhammad, by which faithful Muslims try to lead their lives). After they had collated Jesus' sayings, Matthew's followers then translated the account as best as they could into the Greek texts we have now.

The theory of an older Aramaic version of Matthew's account fits with his gospel being the most obviously Jewish of the four, presenting Jesus as a teacher and lawgiver. Matthew might therefore be expected to give the closest account to that of the modern liberal fantasy Jesus, but we will see that it does not really come close.

35

In case you happen to have religious conversations with an educated Muslim, it might be helpful at this point to share a few things about the Islamic teaching on Jesus. Muslims suppose Jesus to have been just one of many previous prophets, including Adam and Abraham among them, who bore the same ultimate message (or *risalah*) which would ultimately be delivered to Muhammad in the Qur'an. It is alleged that God dictated a book to Jesus called the *Injil*, probably an Arabic rendition of the Greek "Evangelion," which means the Gospel. Islam teaches that this original gospel was lost, and that the four which we Christians have are erroneous, too much of the sense having been lost in transmission. Hence, they say, the inconsistencies in the account. It is because all the ancient books, including the whole Bible, are so inconsistent and corrupt that God gave Muhammad the words of the Qur'an: to set right what had been lost in translation over the centuries.

Now, the lost "Aramaic version" of Matthew under discussion might seem good ammunition for the Muslim cause here. So, it is worth stressing that first, there is *no historical evidence* that Jesus himself wrote such a book, or anything else, for that matter: the only reference in the Bible to Jesus doing anything like writing is when he scribbles with a finger in the sand at the stoning of the woman accused of adultery (John 8:6-8). And actually, even this story does not really prove that Jesus could write, since the Greek verb used could equally mean 'draw.' Anyway, Papias insists that it was *Matthew* who jotted down what Jesus had said and then put it into order, not Jesus himself.

36

The existence of an Aramaic *Injīl* entrusted to Jesus may be an article of Muslim faith, but enjoys no credible historical evidence.

One much later pseudo-gospel called the Gospel of Barnabas does partially match the Islamic view of Jesus as a prophet who ultimately escaped crucifixion, but the earliest manuscripts we have of this date only to the 14th century. There are good reasons therefore to be sceptical at the Islamic suggestion of an 'original' gospel, especially if it comes with claims that Jesus wrote it himself.

Let us leave Matthew, and move on now from the synoptic gospels to St John and his idiosyncratic account. As the youngest apostle, John would certainly still have been alive when Mark, Matthew and Luke-Acts were written. Current scholarship has no reason to dispute the tradition of the Church that John was very young when Jesus was alive, and therefore quite feasibly alive at the time of the writing of the fourth gospel which bears his name.

Scholars tend to agree that the "Johannine" works — that is, John's gospel, the letters attributed to John and the book of Revelation (pedants note: there is no such book in the Bible as "Revelations" with an "s" at the end) — were written by a single school of John's immediate followers. Most agree that this John was the 'beloved disciple' mentioned in that Gospel as reclining on Jesus' chest at the Last Supper and beating Peter to the empty tomb.

Somewhat controversially, Bauckham, on the basis of his work on Papias, instead identifies him with the lesser-known John the Presbyter or Priest, known to posterity in the legend of "Prester John." Bauckham shows how the author of John's gospel draws on the testimony of Peter he has read in Mark, but trumps it with the more direct eyewitness testimony he has heard from John.

Whether the gospel is based on the testimony of the Apostle John or Presbyter John makes little difference to the point here. What matters to us is that it explains the differences between John's account and that of the synoptics. The synoptics are based more or less on Peter's account, which was first hand to Mark, second-hand to Luke and Matthew; but the compiler of John had to square this with the conflicting testimony of the living eyewitness before him: John, in his old age.

If Bauckham is right — and his thesis has certainly been very well received by eminent biblical scholars — this means that despite its relative tardiness, John's gospel is at least as valuable a piece of evidence as the other Gospels about Jesus' contemporaries' testimony about him. It is just different.

The Baptism of the Lord

Let's try to put all this information together now into practice by looking at a specific story of Jesus. We will focus on the first story of his adult life, his Baptism, partly because the stories about his childhood appear only in Luke and to a lesser extent Matthew; and partly because the Baptism is the first public event in his life, which happened immediately before the calling of the first Apostles at Capernaum. This makes it the first recorded event within reach of the living memory of the eye witnesses whose notes would be edited into the gospels.

First, a note of caution: history and testimony cannot be separated. Please discard the notion now that we are going to find an 'historical Jesus' hiding behind the curtain of the Apostles' testimony. It is a fool's game to try to separate an ancient fact (or any fact) from people's perceptions of that fact. The way we see anything is already pre-conditioned by the kind of person we are and the expectations we have of it. Knowing, for example, that a rainbow has eight colours, when you look at a rainbow, you will see eight colours. Yet people from certain African cultures know perfectly well that a rainbow has five colours, and that is how many they see. Aristotle was utterly convinced that a rainbow had only three colours. Contrary to the Dickensian character of Mr Gradgrind and his modern utilitarian analogues, there are simply no such things as 'bare facts,' empty of human speculation and expectation.

"facts" & perception

This is why the expectations of the various eyewitnesses who saw Jesus matter so much. They certainly were not "neutral"— but who is? Recognition of the inevitable subjectivity of history means that it is quite impossible to understand Jesus without understanding the context of the gospels and the expectations of their authors.

St Peter, for instance, expected something quite different from what he ultimately got: he wanted a warrior Messiah. Nor was he the only one. The Gospel of Mark in particular is a catalogue of the disciples' mistakes and failures to see Jesus for what he was. So if the gospels are truly based on eyewitness testimony, what this means is that the disciples' failure *is being acknowledged by the disciples themselves.* The self-deprecation of the disciples hardly seems to fit the modern fiction of the early Church as some cabal of self-interested powermongers, desperate to establish its supremacy by spreading whatever lies they could about its founder.

In any case, by the time the eyewitnesses gave their testimony, Jesus had already died and — his followers claimed — risen. We can therefore read the gospels only on the basis that those who describe events are doing so in retrospect, and with the conviction that Jesus had risen from the dead. As we have seen from Paul's letters, these Apostles were the leaders of a growing, organized Church which from the earliest times maintained that Jesus was the Son of God and universal saviour.

What this means is that the Church must take logical priority over the gospels, and in fact, over Scripture as a whole: the Church had to exist before it could give us the Bible.

What is more, the Bible was authoritative only because the Church decided so. In the words of a letter against the Manichaean heresy written by the great 4th century North African bishop St Augustine, "I would not believe the Gospel unless moved thereto by the authority of the Church."

This being so, the only way to make any sense of the gospels is to read them under the assumptions of the faith their writers shared, including *faith in the Church which Jesus had founded* with the Apostles as its

Iconography as meaning theology

foundations. Attempts at demythologisation, earnest entreaties to let the Bible speak for itself without reference to the Church which gave it birth, or appeals to supposedly common sense ideas of Jesus as a liberal or radical rabbi will only distort the picture. Separate Jesus from the witness of his Church, and you have practically nothing left.

Icons of the Baptism of Christ like the one below can help to explain what I mean about reading the Bible in the context of the Church. In this iconographical tradition, the locale of Jesus' baptism is portrayed as a sort of cavern, which represents neither the gospel narratives nor the geography of the River Jordan. So, is this a prime example of the Church distorting the Gospel for its own purposes?

Of course, you would expect me by now to say "no." The Church is depicting Jesus' baptism like this for two reasons.

First, we know from archaeological evidence that early Christian baptisms were conducted in cave-like baptisteries underneath or outside the main body of the church building. So the image of Christ's baptism in a cavern identifies it in the faithful Christian's mind with his or her own baptism.

And second, before you start objecting that baptisms should be done out in rivers just like Jesus' was, there is a very sound symbolic reason for the baptism to take place in a cave, echoing symbolism which is found in the Gospel accounts themselves.

Compare the icon of the Baptism of Christ with an icon of his descent into Hell. You will see that hell

41

Baptism of Christ

is represented as a very similar sort of cave to the baptism scene.

Now this is not related in the stories of the gospels, told straight as stories. Rather, the iconographers are drawing on the wider theological implications of Scripture as whole, especially the thought of St Paul. In their icons, the baptistery becomes a foreshadowing of the underworld.

This is not a later Church innovation, but is woven into the gospel accounts themselves. Luke's account of the baptism, in chapter 3, begins by bringing up the spectres of Herod, Pontius Pilate and Cai-

Harrowing of Hell

aphas, so cleverly linking Jesus' Baptism with his death on the Cross. He makes the Baptism a foreshadowing of the Cross.

Later, in a mirror image of this, Luke 12.50 has Jesus describe his forthcoming death as a baptism: "I have a baptism to be baptized with; and how I am constrained until it is accomplished!" That last word will echo in the ears of hearers of St John's account of the Passion, for John makes it Jesus' very last word of all. And so, for those with ears to hear, the Cross becomes a kind of Baptism. You can find a similar reference in Mark 10.38.

None of this would surprise hearers of the gospels if they had heard or read what Paul had already written on the subject some years ago in his letter to the Romans:

"Do you not know that all of us who have been baptized into Christ Jesus were baptized into his death? We were buried therefore with him by baptism into death, so that as Christ was raised from the dead by the glory of the Father, we too might walk in newness of life. For if we have been united with him in a death like his, we shall certainly be united with him in a resurrection like his." (Romans 6:3-5)

In St John's gospel account of the Baptism, St John the Baptist famously calls Jesus "the Lamb of God" (John 1.36), linking Jesus' Baptism directly to his sacrificial death. Yet taken chronologically, this had already been established as a motif in the letters of Paul:

"Cleanse out the old leaven that you may be a new lump, as you really are unleavened. For Christ, our paschal lamb, has been sacrificed." (1 Corinthians 5.7)

St Peter himself had made the same connection in his letter written some four decades before the Gospel according to St John:

"You know that you were ransomed from the futile ways inherited from your fathers, not with perishable things such as silver or gold, but with the precious blood of Christ, like that of a lamb without blemish or spot." (1 Peter 1.18-19)

The early representation of the Gospel in Church iconography shows a sophisticated and many-layered understanding of the Scriptures. The example above only gives one small insight into the interwoven meanings and readings of this hermeneutic tapestry.

Such subtlety can also be found in the writings of the early Church Fathers, whose works have lain unread by most Christians for far too long, but are happily now readily available in paperback editions and read throughout Christian denominations. Their importance is testified to by the fact that so much of their work is prescribed for reading in early morning prayers of the Divine Office, the book of daily prayer which all priests and religious are canonically bound to recite and in which the laity are strongly encouraged to participate. The Fathers' insight, the insight of the first few centuries of Christians, is indispensable for understanding who Jesus was.

The Gospels, we can more or less safely say, were based substantially on the testimony of eyewitnesses, and those eyewitnesses were already members, indeed leaders, of the Church. They had been baptized as Christ was baptized, and Peter and Paul's letters show how from early days they understood Our Lord's baptism in the light of their own baptism and of his Crucifixion. It makes no sense, then, to try to unpick a pristine, unadulterated Jesus out from their interwoven accounts.

Nor, ultimately, do we need to: for the simple reason that Jesus chose those eyewitnesses, the Apostles, himself. They did not appoint themselves. Their understanding of Jesus, the understanding of those men whom Jesus himself chose to be the foundation stones of the Church, is what we find recorded in the gospels, which are written in continuity with the beliefs we found in the earlier Christian writings of Paul.

The only question which remains is to what extent we trust the witness of the Apostles: which amounts to asking, do we trust the witness of the Church? If not, as Augustine pointed out, we have no real reason to believe a word of the Gospel.

There are at least two compelling reasons why one might trust the testimony of the Apostles. The first only applies to those who find Jesus trustworthy, and it is straightforward: if we trust Jesus, then we should trust that he appointed honest followers to succeed him. But of course, this is a circular argument unlikely to persuade anyone who is not already convinced of Jesus' worth.

The second reason to trust the Apostles requires no such faith. On the Apostles' feast days, traditional churches will dress their altars and clergy in red, to represent their blood. This is because the Apostles ended up as martyrs. There was no end of mystery religions that the Apostles could have joined after Jesus died, if they were looking for promises of enlightenment and eternal life: legitimate, pagan cults which would not have demanded their untimely and often gruesome deaths at the hands of the authorities. And yet, the Apostles persisted in their belief that Christ had died and risen, and was indeed God the Word made flesh, even at the expense of their lives. They may have been mistaken in their belief, but I for one consider this strong evidence that they really did believe in what they professed. Truly the seed of the

Church was sown in the blood of the martyrs, the Apostles among them.

Without the witness of the Apostles, there is really nothing to be said of Jesus at all. He becomes a remote and barely sketched figure in the shadows of long past history. It turns out that the only Jesus we have any access to is the Jesus of the Church, the Jesus who is portrayed as Son of God and Saviour: the risen Jesus who revealed himself to Paul and whom even the earliest Christians treated as "equal to God."

They were either right to treat Jesus this way, or they were blasphemers and idolaters. There is no middle way, no secular humanist Christianity – I am glad to say, given the destruction that the individualism implicit in secular humanism continues to wreak among nations and families, and especially among the poor. Even the words that the most Jewish version of Jesus says of himself, the Jesus of Matthew's Gospel, resolutely refuse to conform to this modern model.

So, it is to Matthew's most Jewish Jesus that we next turn.

5. THE JEWISH JESUS

St Matthew's is generally regarded as the most Jewish of the four gospels. He famously represents Jesus as a great teacher or 'rabbi.'

So, out of any of the them, we might expect Matthew's biography of Jesus to conform most strongly to the Monty Python version of Jesus as "not the Messiah, just a very naughty boy," and definitely not God. After all, Judaism is known for its resolute monotheism, so surely Matthew of all the evangelists is the least likely to attribute divinity to Christ.

In the last chapter, I argued that we can read the gospels, written rather later, only in the light of the basic Christian assumptions of Jesus' equality with God that we find in the early letters of Paul. There is no hope of reaching some sort of pristine 'historical' Jesus who dwells inaccessibly 'behind' the Church's texts of the New Testament: in fact, it seems a fool's quest even to try to do so, since all history is conditioned by the interpretation of those who experience and relate it. That said, we saw that the time lapse between the death of Jesus and the writing of the Gospels by no means precludes their having been written on the basis of living eyewitness testimony, as Professor Bauckham's work compellingly testifies.

The Gospels of Mark, written around AD 70, and Luke (with its sequel, Acts), written ten or so years later, were arguably based on the testimony of St Peter. St John's Gospel, committed to writing far later, seems to be based on that recorded testimony, but also on the living and somewhat different account of either John the Apostle himself or John the Presbyter, younger contemporaries of Jesus. All three of these accounts describe Jesus as divine. Luke does so more weakly than the others, and John, the latest, is most explicit in proclaiming Jesus' divinity.

The Gospel according to St Matthew is the one with the least clearly defined eyewitness pedigree. It was written around the same time as Luke and Acts, but unlike their orientation towards a more gentile audience, Matthew offers a more obviously Jewish slant. The second-century disciple of John called Papias tells us that this gospel was a translation of "logia," recorded sayings of Jesus, which Matthew himself noted down in Aramaic: a student's notes, if you like. It is not so much based on the continuous narrative of Peter or of John as on a collection of sayings of Jesus. So even if we cannot get at a purely objective account of Jesus (any more than we can get at a purely objective account of Julius Caesar or Winston Churchill, for that matter), perhaps his collected sayings in this gospel will give us a view of him more consistent with the popular opinion of Jesus as an extraordinary rabbi of yore and nothing more.

Jesus and the Torah

The most important aspect of mainstream Jewish faith in Jesus' day, as now, was the Torah or "Law." This is the first part of the Jewish scriptures, which Christians call the Old Testament. It comprises the first five books, which gives them the alternative Greek name of the "Pentateuch." The Torah is traditionally ascribed to Moses, though impossibly: he could not actually have written them, partly because they describe his own death.

Like the New Testament, the order of the books in the table of contents has very little to do with their order of composition: in fact, the Torah, including Genesis, the Laws and the creation stories, were written down two or three centuries later than some of the Prophets and historical Writings.

Leaving that aside, Jews of Jesus' time believed that the Law was given by God to Moses on Mount Sinai (or Mount Horeb). The Law was the word of God, and following it was the recipe for a life pleasing to him. Certainly, for the Pharisees at least, there was no room (in the language of the King James version of the Bible) for even 'a jot or tittle' of the Law to be changed: a 'jot' is an older English word for the smallest letter of the Greek alphabet, *iota*, and a 'tittle' means a punctuation mark. Still, even such small changes could radically alter the meaning of the text.

So, we can understand why Matthew's Jesus is adamant that he does not intend to change the Law at all:

> "Think not that I have come to abolish the law and the prophets; I have come not to abolish them but to

fulfil them. For truly, I say to you, till heaven and earth pass away, not an iota, not a dot, will pass from the law until all is accomplished. Whoever then relaxes one of the least of these commandments and teaches men so, shall be called least in the kingdom of heaven; but he who does them and teaches them shall be called great in the kingdom of heaven. For I tell you, unless your righteousness exceeds that of the scribes and Pharisees, you will never enter the kingdom of heaven." (Matthew 5:17-20)

It looks, then, like Jesus is calling his disciples to follow the Law just as any conservative rabbi might. And yet, he follows this firm statement of orthodoxy with a series of, to put it mildly, "reinterpretations."

If you look at Matthew 5:21 onwards, you will see a whole series of statements beginning "you have heard that it was said." This is a typical rabbinic idiom, where the word "said" means "interpreted," in the sense of a rabbi giving proper interpretation to the Scriptures. So far, so rabbinic.

Jesus then does something controversial: he takes each law far beyond the limits that logic or reason require, and pushes each law to absurd extents. The authority by which he does this is not Scripture itself, not the Torah, not even the traditional assent of fellow rabbis, but – here is the shocking innovation – the authority is *himself*. "You have heard that it was said," he begins each instance: "but I say to you."

Jesus is saying, "I, Jesus, have the authority to define divine Law." He is putting *himself* in the place of the God-given Torah tablets and scrolls, making *himself* the Law. You can see why this might be problematic.

There are plenty of examples of Jesus' extreme interpretations of Torah in his Sermon on the Mount, but let us focus on just one of these, in Matthew 5.21-22. Note again how he begins with that characteristically rabbinical phrase and then makes himself the authority:

> "*You have heard* that it was said to the men of old, 'You shall not kill; and whoever kills shall be liable to judgment.' *But I say* to you that every one who is angry with his brother shall be liable to judgment; whoever insults his brother shall be liable to the council, and whoever says, 'You fool!' shall be liable to the hell of fire."

Look at the extreme to which Jesus is pushing this law. If you regularly attend church or read the Bible, there is a danger that overfamiliarity with this often-read text might dull you to the scandal of what Jesus is saying.

Anyone might agree with the law as it stands: do not kill people, a common prohibition throughout human history and cultures. But what do we make of Jesus' interpretation? He says that anyone who is even angry with his 'brother' — which can mean any male relative, in fact — anyone who even insults his brother, or calls him a 'raka,' an insult meaning 'piece of spittle,' is liable to judgment before the council and the hell of fire.

Perhaps a little harsh. Or even *impossibly* harsh. Look further down the page of the Bible, and you will see that the rest of Jesus' counsel is likewise extreme:

• If you have ever so much as glanced at a woman in lust, you are an adulterer and should cut out your eye.

• If you divorce your wife, you make her an adulteress.

• It is not just wrong but evil to swear an oath.

• If someone hits you on the cheek, give him the other one to hit, too.

Interesting, as an aside, how some Christians take one or two of these interpretations so much more seriously than the rest. Christians need to keep asking whether our priorities are the same as Jesus', and importantly need to be aware of the context of his words.

For instance, saying 'God is great' means one thing after the safe delivery of a child; it means quite another when smashing in the head of an infidel during a crusade.

One could even quote the Bible to say, 'there is no God.' It's there in the first line of Psalm 14— if you leave out the first part of the sentence, 'the fool says in his heart.' Picking out proof texts is a dangerous pastime: context is everything.

So, to put this passage into context, Jesus began by saying, "unless your righteousness exceeds that of the scribes and Pharisees, you will never enter the kingdom of heaven" (Matthew 20). That word, "righteousness," is a technical term in the Old Testament which mainstream Judaism interpreted as "fidelity to the Torah." So, the Jewish Jesus is telling his disciples they will not enter the kingdom of heaven unless they "are more faithful to the Torah (the Law) than the scribes and Pharisees:" that is, even more faithful to the Law than the lawyers.

But it is the end of the passage which really shows how Jesus wants us to understand it:

"Love your enemy, because you must be perfect just as God is perfect."

Jesus is telling the disciples to be "perfect," even as God is perfect.

To be as perfect as God.

Mainstream Jews and Muslims would object that humans cannot be as perfect as God. And Christians would have to agree: not by our own efforts, at any rate.

But worse, can we even hope by our own efforts to be able to live up to Jesus' high moral demands?

Surely not. We cannot be as faithful to the Torah as Jesus wants us to, we cannot exceed the Pharisees and Scribes. I know that I am not the only one who has in my lifetime fallen foul many times of at least one of these extreme interpretations of righteousness. I have not managed to maintain absolute fidelity to the Law.

So, then, I too must be condemned by Jesus to the fiery Hell.

Hopelessness would be the conclusion we would have to draw, I think, if this were the only part of Matthew's Gospel to have survived. Fortunately, it is not, and if we look deeper into who Jesus claims to be, we will see how Christians still have a great hope: far greater than our own vain attempts at keeping impossible laws could ever give us.

Jesus: lawbreaker or lawmaker?

Matthew's Jesus draws the Pharisees' attention to the impossibility of saving themselves from damnation by their vain attempts at adhering to the Law, a warning which extends just as much to Christians today.

So what, exactly, does this rabbi prescribe for the salvation of humankind?

To be sure, it will have nothing to do with secular assumptions about being 'a good person' whether one is religious or not, because Jesus has just told us that our own efforts to be good, in themselves, will get us nowhere. Christianity is not a religion of 'values.' Unless we cooperate in God's work, we are building our house on sand. Our Lord was definitely not preaching the modern gospel professed by the burgeoning trade in self-help manuals.

Jesus' approach to the Law gives us an insight into its limitations: or to put it more properly, our human limitations in regard to observing the law. Let us look at another of Jesus' "reinterpretations," this time of the Sabbath:

> "At that time Jesus went through the grainfields on the sabbath; his disciples were hungry, and they began to pluck heads of grain and to eat. But when the Pharisees saw it, they said to him, 'Look, your disciples are doing what is not lawful to do on the sabbath.'

> "He said to them, 'Have you not read what David did, when he was hungry, and those who were with him: how he entered the house of God and ate the bread of the Presence, which it was not lawful for him to eat nor for those who were with him, but only for the priests? Or have you not read in the law how on the

sabbath the priests in the Temple profane the sabbath, and are guiltless? I tell you, something greater than the Temple is here. And if you had known what this means, *I desire mercy, and not sacrifice,* you would not have condemned the guiltless. For the Son of man is lord of the sabbath.'" (Matthew 12:1-8)

This story is often taken at Sunday school level (and in some churches, I fear, in the sermons for grown-ups, too) to show the contrast between those wicked, Pharisaical sticklers for pointless old tradition, as opposed to the wonderful pragmatism of the liberal Jesus.

This interpretation woefully misrepresents the importance of the Sabbath to Jewish piety and spirituality. The Sabbath is not just an exercise of morality or self-restraint, but an *imitation of God in his work of creation resting on the seventh day.*

In traditional Jewish understanding, the seventh day, the day of Sabbath rest, is not just a break from work. It is, if you like, an icon of the fundamental goal of creation itself: God created everything not for work, but so that it would ultimately be at rest in him. The Sabbath is meant to be a taste of heaven, a day of prayer and gentle repose in God. More's the pity many Christian churches have all but abolished that understanding, even to the extent that the trendier and more "progressive" elements no longer see collective Sunday worship as mandatory or even "helpful:" better, they say, if everyone just turns up when it's convenient to them. Well, better than nothing, for sure. But it would be a mistake to read Jesus in this passage as endorsing such an individualistic view.

The point of this story is not that Jesus is a law-breaker seeking to break down tradition, but that he is, as he calls himself, "greater than the Temple" and "Lord of the Sabbath."

Given what I've just said about the Sabbath, you can see what a shocking statement that is. Jesus is not claiming to be "Lord of the day off." He is claiming to be Lord of the seventh day, Lord of the coming of heaven here in earth, Lord of the ultimate goal of all Creation.

This, he says, is because he (possibly along with his disciples) is "greater than the Temple"— where, we must remember, Jesus' contemporaries firmly believed God was, in some way, really present, and which was also the house of the sacred Torah scrolls.

Jesus has said, remember, that anyone who relaxes any of the Law will be least in the Kingdom of Heaven. So, he cannot possibly see himself as breaking the Law here, when he and his disciples appear to be breaking the Sabbath. Indeed, he claims to be "guilt-less." But the reason that he — and, by association, his disciples — are guiltless is not because of a rabbinical contest about the niceties of the Law, but because of who Jesus claims to be: Lord of the Sabbath, greater than the Temple, the very dwelling place of God.

This gives us one major clue as to why Jesus' disciples are not resigned to hopelessness after all, despite the impossibility of the Law that hangs over them. Jesus defends his disciples against the lawyers, the Pharisees, purely on the grounds of their association with him. This defence works only if Jesus is something rather more special than a roaming rabbi.

A further clue can be found in another of Jesus' apparently tearaway moments, when he might seem to the untrained eye to be tearing apart tradition.

Christian family values

Commentators are wont to mutter darkly about the erosion of "Christian family values."

To a great extent I sympathize with their sentiment. The world and especially the poor urgently need a return to the stability of deeply loving families which only unconditional bonds, blessed and nurtured by God's power, can hope to provide.

It is the method that I take issue with. Any attempt to reduce the content of the Christian revelation to a set of 'values' which can be extracted from an actual relationship with the person of Jesus Christ is as doomed to failure as the Pharisaical attempts to adhere to Law outlined above. Christian values come from a living Christian faith, from regular confession and hearing of mass, from an engaged and disciplined prayer life. They cannot simply be taken as a moral code to be imposed: they must be learnt and loved in the experience of the God-fearing human heart. That is where Christian families will find their nurture.

It may be something of a stereotype to say how much family matters to Jews, but I think my Jewish friends would concede that it is not an unfair one. In Jesus' own day, family mattered more to the Sadducees than to the Pharisees: because the former did not believe in any resurrection, the only way to live on after death was through one's offspring, hence the importance of 'going forth and multiplying.'

This may be part of the origin of the importance Islam has historically placed on marriage and procreation. The Islamic model has much in common with conservative Christian, especially Protestant, understandings about family, too: the sense that it is a Christian duty to have a family was part of the reason for abolishing the requirement of celibacy among the clergy at the Reformation.

Yet there are several texts in Matthew which are not so easily to reconcile with the ancient Jewish or modern conservative preoccupation with family. Jesus once again takes us to the extremes of the Torah:

> "While he was still speaking to the people, behold, his mother and his brethren stood outside, asking to speak to him. But he replied to the man who told him, 'Who is my mother, and who are my brethren?' And stretching out his hand toward his disciples, he said, 'Here are my mother and my brethren! For whoever does the will of my Father in heaven is my brother, and sister, and mother.'" (Matthew 12.46-50)

Here Jesus extends the notion of family to all those who follow God's will. This can be read as a positive view of the family; for by saying that his disciples are his family, Jesus is indicating that family is to be regarded as a good thing.

The same cannot be said, though, of another more radical passage, which considerably relativizes the family's importance against the importance of relationship with Jesus himself:

"I have come to set a man against his father, and a daughter against her mother, and a daughter-in-law against her mother-in-law; and a man's foes will be those of his own household. He who loves father or mother more than me is not worthy of me; and he who loves son or daughter more than me is not worthy of me." (Matthew 10.35-37)

These words show that the value of celibacy is at least as important as that of family, which would as be as scandalous an idea to an ancient rabbi as it would to a modern Muslim or certain stripe of modern Christian. Worse, to the ears of such a fellow rabbi, either of these sayings would seem to fall far short of Jesus' professed rigour in observing the Law, bearing in mind the Ten Commandments:

"Honour your father and your mother, so that your days may be long in the land that the Lord your God is giving you." (Exodus 20.12)

If Jesus is nothing more than an exceptional rabbi, then here he is breaking the Law again, just as he would have been breaking the Law of the Sabbath had he been just a rabbi. That, indeed, is a substantial part of the reason that his fellow rabbis plotted against him.

The key to understanding how Jesus can appear simultaneously to counsel strict adherence to the Law and to break it here is the idea that he is the Son of God. Then, the Torah principle of honouring one's parents is given deeper significance: it means obedience to the divine Father, God.

One might argue at this point that surely, anyone could make this claim to be a child of God. Jesus' words here do not imply that he is uniquely the Son of God, the only one. Indeed, if we took this passage in isolation, you could make that argument. But we have to take it in connexion with Matthew's portrait of Jesus as a whole. We have to look at how he positions himself in relation to the Law, to Torah, in the widest possible sense.

We saw first, that Jesus told his disciples not only that they must keep the Law, but that they must do so even more rigorously than the Pharisees, with all sorts of impossible injunctions; second, that they must do so to the impossible extent of being as perfect as God the Father; third, that for them, it is Jesus' personal interpretation of the Law which is binding; fourth, that it is binding not because of what he says, but because of who he is and his personal authority; fifth, that his disciples are authorised to follow his interpretations of the Law because together with him, they constitute something greater than the Temple, so great that he can proclaim himself "Lord of the Sabbath," with the power even to reinterpret and overrule the Temple's most sacred religious precept, the day of Sabbath rest.

Take Jesus' apparently unorthodox outbursts about family in light of all this, and we start to see the nature of the qualification, as it were, to Jesus' impossible demands.

The qualification is *membership of Jesus' family*.

But not membership of his blood family – one's blood has nothing to do with one's righteousness in the economy of salvation that Jesus is announcing. It is only by adoption with Jesus as a fellow son or daughter of his heavenly Father that one can fulfil the requirements of the Law as Jesus interprets it: hence, "whoever does the will of my Father in heaven is my brother, and sister, and mother."

Jesus the New Moses

The Law as Jesus interprets it remains impossible for us to fulfil. So, for all this, we are still left with one gaping hole in the jigsaw. Who can make the impossible possible?

To that question, there is only one answer, which Jesus answers in relation to rich people being saved and camels passing through the eyes of needles:

> "But Jesus looked at them and said to them, 'With men this is impossible, but *with God* all things are possible.'" (Matthew 19:26)

Only God can make the impossible possible.

And yet perhaps the most important facet of Matthew's Jesus, without nothing else about Jesus would really make any sense, is that he *does* achieve the impossible, that which the Scriptures and even Jesus himself make absolutely clear is impossible.

It is no coincidence that Jesus' most famous sermon, recorded in Matthew 5 onwards, was delivered from what has traditionally been designated a "mount." The reality of the place is that it was a low hill just outside Capernaum, but the reason Matthew want to call it a "mount" is to make a parallel with Moses, who in Jewish tradition ascended Mount Sinai to receive the Law from God. There, it is said, Moses *heard* God: but what he could not do was *look at* God:

"'But,' [the Lord] said, 'you cannot see my face; for *man shall not see me and live.*' And the Lord said, 'Behold, there is a place by me where you shall stand upon the rock; and while my glory passes by I will put you in a cleft of the rock, and I will cover you with my hand until I have passed by; then I will take away my hand, and you shall see my back; but my face *shall not be seen.*'" (Exodus 33.20-23)

When Jesus gives the Law from his respective "mount," echoing Moses, he blatantly contradicts this, saying, "Blessed are the pure in heart, for they *shall see* God." (Matthew 5:8)

Once again, we are left with Jesus uttering a paradox that seems to oppose at least the mainstream Jewish tradition of his time. There were other Jewish traditions in Jesus' time which were more open to the possibility of seeing God, notably unearthed in the twentieth century discovery of scrolls in Qumran.

Margaret Barker, a Methodist scholar of the Old Testament, has written extensively on what she calls the tradition of "Temple Mysticism," which she argues was deliberately edited out of the Jewish scriptures by the prominent rabbis of the early Christian period because it made so much sense of Christian claims about Jesus. She says that a strand of Judaism based firmly on Deuteronomy, and with it the impossibility of 'seeing God,' became the exclusively dominant form of the religion only *after* Jesus' death and in the early days of the Church. The tradition of Temple Mysticism was less dogmatically monotheistic than 'Deuteronomistic' Judaism, permitting a greater role of mediation between God and creation, particularly through angels. Much of the extra-biblical literature in the days of the early Church gives Jesus 'angelic' characteristics.

Jesus was therefore most likely speaking within a particular tradition of Judaism, but one which survives now only in its Christian form. To his fellow followers, his claims could be reconciled with their rich view of the divinely infused universe, which gave birth to Catholic doctrine about angels and the company of saints. But to his detractors, those who held to the dominant, law-based form of the faith, Jesus was making claims to a divine status which were nothing short of heretical.

Jesus' claims make no sense unless Matthew believed him to share in God's divinity in a special way. If Jesus was speaking without the authority of the Father, the authority given only to a first-born son, then he was provoking his disciples to extreme disobedience against God: not only in the minutiae of prescriptive laws, but even in our fundamental relationship to God through his Temple, through the hallowed time of the Sabbath, and now even in direct face-to-face contact with God. Jesus is making the extraordinary claim that, through him, we can know the unknowable. If we know him, we know the Father.

All this places Matthew's Jesus far from the liberal or even radical rabbi of modern supposition. Jesus puts himself in the place of the Law, the Temple, even the Sabbath. This contributes to the sense of the Trinitarian teaching that Jesus is God's incarnate Word, even though the doctrine of the Trinity proper would not be fully articulated for some time yet. His nature as divine Word is what authorises him to re-define the parameters of the Law; his nature as Son of God authorizes him to draw people into the saving relationship he has with the Father through adoption into his family, the Church.

None of this makes any sense unless Matthew believed that Jesus was indeed the divine Son of God, and that the rest of us could be adopted to participate in his sonship. So it is that not by our own efforts, but by participation in his relationship to the Father, we might come to join him in seeing God face-to-face. Then the Law will be written not on scrolls or external tablets of stone, but in our hearts, as it is in Jesus'.

It is reasonable to presume that Matthew knew the ancient Christian hymn which we found in Paul's letter to the Philippians. It may provide us with a hermeneutic key to unlock some of the mystery of the paradoxical Jesus whose portrait Matthew paints, and so I quote it again:

> "Have this mind among yourselves, which is yours in Christ Jesus, who, though he was in the form of God, did not count equality with God a thing to be grasped, but emptied himself, taking the form of a servant, being born in the likeness of men. And being found in human form he humbled himself and became obedient unto death, even death on a cross." (Philippians 2.5-11)

Christians are not supposed to believe that we can of our own devices do any of the impossible things that Jesus demands of us. We can do them only because Jesus has done them— or, putting it more accurately, because Jesus is the living embodiment of them. We can be pure of heart and so see the Father only by having the "mind of Christ," decreasing in ourselves so that he might increase in us, letting him adopt us as his brothers and sisters, relying entirely on his Incarnation, Crucifixion and glorious Ascension for our "justification" by God – which is to say, to be restored to our proper place before him. Only God can do what Jesus claimed that he could do for us.

That is why the Pharisees wanted to kill him. Do you really think they would have bothered if he were just a liberal rabbi?

6. THE DEVIL'S JESUS

"All scripture is inspired by God and profitable for teaching, for reproof, for correction, and for training in righteousness." (2 Timothy 3:16)

Ask a biblical fundamentalist to justify belief in the Bible as the inerrant, literal word of God, and the above *bon mot* attributed to St Paul is likely to be the stock response.

If we were starting from the position that Christianity is all about the Bible and nothing else, then I suppose it might sound pretty convincing. But given what we have covered so far, I hope you can see there are some problems with this idea.

Think back to Chapter 1, when we put the New Testament in chronological order. The earliest texts were St Paul's letters. So what does that imply about the statement in the second letter to Timothy about "Scripture"— what can the word "Scripture" be referring to? Or a prior question: what must it *not* be referring to?

Well, for a start, it cannot be referring to the gospels, Acts and many of the letters. These had not yet been written, so the writer (possibly St Paul himself, possibly a disciple of his) cannot be referring to them as "scripture." Nor does anything in his own writing suggest that Paul thought his own letters were or would ever be considered part of sacred scripture.

That rules out the entire New Testament, then.

So, what the author of 2 Timothy is referring to must be the Old Testament (more or less— for reasons I will come back to). But even then, he does not write that "*only* Scripture is God-breathed;" his statement does not imply at all that the Scriptures as they stand are conclusive, or that God does not speak outside them: for instance, through the tradition of the Church.

Nor for that matter, does the author say, "Scripture is divinely *dictated.*" The Greek word he uses is *theopneustos*, "God-breathed," "God inspired," or even in a sense "divine-spirited:" the Holy Spirit, in Greek, is the *hagios pneuma*. Spirit, *pneuma*, and the latter half of *theo-pneustos* are cognate (that is, they come from the same word family), along with our word 'pneumatic.' So what Paul is saying is that the scriptures of the Old Testament are *infused with the Spirit of God*. That is not the same thing as saying that they are "divinely dictated" or "infallible."

In the final analysis, the Scriptures cannot be the only things that are infused with God's Spirit or breath. The first and foremost Word breathed from God's mouth is *Jesus Christ himself*, the Word made Flesh, as St John's Gospel particularly attests. Then, the Church that Jesus founded and left behind as his Body was imbued with the Spirit at Pentecost, again according to the Scriptures (Acts in this case). So: *the*

Christian Scriptures were 'breathed out' only subsequently to Jesus and the Church.

The thrust of my argument has been that we cannot understand the Scriptures without reference to the Church which formed them, and so cannot understand Jesus without reference to the Church he formed, since we have any knowledge of Jesus at all only through the Scriptures, which the Church was inspired to write. The very earliest Christians believed in Jesus as equal to God and as saviour of the world, and the Gospels, although written rather later, were written within living memory of some of the Apostles, based on the recorded eyewitness testimony of others, and they too show the early Church's belief in Jesus as divine. Even the most Jewish portrait of Jesus — Matthew's — failed to match modern ideas of strict Jewish monotheism, wary of asserting Jesus' divinity, and gave us nothing to support the idea of Jesus as just a charismatic liberal or radical rabbi. On the contrary, if Jesus' followers were at all accurate in reporting what he said, by making himself arbiter of the Torah and Lord of the Sabbath, Jesus put himself where only God belonged.

An important implication of all this is that *the Church takes logical precedence over the Bible.* We are in grave danger of distorting the meaning of the gospel if we read the New Testament outside the context it was written in, and without the assumptions of the people who wrote it.

Those people, it seems clear from what we have seen so far, believed in and worshipped Jesus with reverence due only to God. They were part of a movement which he had himself established and sent out to proclaim the coming of the Kingdom, to call people to repent and be baptised.

The Pauline epistles, the *Didache* and the evidence of the early Church Fathers also show that the first Christians gathered at least weekly to break bread in remembrance of Jesus' sacrifice on the Cross. They were, in short, that eucharistic community which we call the Church, and we saw that even as early as Paul's first letter to the Thessalonians around AD 50, the Church had some rudimentary form of apostolic order. In other words, the early Christians had order and sacraments — Baptism and the Eucharist, at least — before they had any of their "own" Scriptures, separate from the Greek Old Testament.

Make no mistake, as a Christian priest, I heartily concur with the author of 2 Timothy that "all scripture is inspired by God and profitable for teaching, for reproof, for correction, and for training in righteousness." But I do not think for a moment that it follows from this that the Bible is the be-all-and-end-all of Christianity, or even that Christianity should first and foremost pride itself on being "Bible-based."

In fact, the description of Christians as "People of the Book" is a Muslim designation: it is what the Qur'an calls us. The scholar John Barton conclusively repudiates this description in his book of the same name. The Bible deserves a high place of honour, surely, but not so high that it displaces the fundamental Christian truth of the Incarnation: the Blessed Virgin Mary gave birth to a boy, not a book. We have no conclusive evidence that Jesus ever even wrote a word.

The modern Protestant biblical fundamentalist strategy of taking individual sentences of Scripture to prove doctrinal points derives from an exaggerated and ahistorical view of the Bible. We will see that it makes no sense in terms of the historical formation of the Bible and, worse still, contradicts the Bible's own internal evidence of how Jesus and his early followers used Scripture themselves.

To understand this, we need briefly to explore the formation of "the Bible" as we now know it, and then look at a very telling example from the Bible of how it should *not* be used.

The Formation of the Bible

A quick question: how many books are there in the Bible? Do have a look in your bible if you have one to hand.

If you are reading this book as part of a study group, you are likely to come up with different answers.

It may not have escaped your notice in this book that although I happily write about Scripture, until this chapter I have rarely used the phrase "the Bible." It is a term of which I am wary. This is because I am not convinced that there is such a thing as "the Bible."

Please do not mistake me for saying that there is no Bible! Rather, I am saying that there are many bibles.

Take the Old Testament alone. There are at least five distinct possibilities:

1. *The Jewish and Evangelical Protestant Old Testament:* 24 Hebrew books only.

2. *The Roman Catholic Bible:* 24 canonical Hebrew books interspersed with the 7 Greek books which appear in the Septuagint but not in the Hebrew scriptures considered "deutero-canonical:" a "secondary canon," but authoritative in establishing doctrine.

3. *The Greek Orthodox Bible:* as the Roman Catholic Bible, plus 3 extra Greek books and one extra Psalm in the deuterocanon.

4. *The Ethiopic Bible:* As the Orthodox, but with two more books.

5. *The Anglican Bible:* 24 Hebrew books regarded as canonical. The Greek Deuterocanon is referred to as "Apocrypha" and additionally recommended in Article 6 of the Church of England's 39 Articles "for example of life and instruction of manners," but not for establishing doctrine.

There is some, though less, variation in the New Testament canon. For example, the Coptic Church recognises two extra books as canonical (1 and 2 Clement). Or take Luther, architect of the first European Reformation, who was so dismissive of James, Hebrews, Jude and Revelation, that he had them printed *after* the rest of the Bible as a sort of unofficial New Testament deuterocanon. They did not fit in well enough with his new doctrines, but he could not bring himself to excise them completely.

So, we see that there is a diversity in opinion of what "the Bible" might be. The reason for this is pretty obvious: there has never been one single authoritative body in the entire Church to enforce one single canon of Scripture. Rather, various authoritative bodies have decided what does or does not fit into the Bible based on their particular theological concerns.

For example, the Church of England chose not to accept the doctrinal authority of the so-called "Apocrypha" partly because, in 2 Maccabees 12.38-45, we find Judas collecting money to make an offering at the Temple in Jerusalem for prayers for his fallen comrades. The Reformers were very much against prayers for the dead. So, that part of the Scriptures which contradicted their novel view was relegated to an "example of life and instruction of manners." Even "Bible-believing" Christianity ends up being very picky about which bits of the Bible are really to be believed, and how.

It was in response to Protestant redefinitions of canon like this that the Catholic Church in the Council of Trent, 1546, declared the *equality* of the deuterocanonical books, those which were written only in Greek, with the Hebrew Scriptures. More recent scholarship shows that the Church was right to do so, as the New Testament refers far more to the Greek Septuagint than it does to the Hebrew scriptures, which were later doctored by the rabbis to avoid Christian connotations as I have previously described. The Septuagint was the version that had been composed around 300 years before Christ in Alexandria simply because even then, most Jews no longer understood Hebrew, and it contained those seven extra books not found in the Hebrew. This was certainly the Bible that St Paul knew.

Still, St Jerome, making the Latin Vulgate translation, chose to use the edited Hebrew version so that the rabbis would have no ammunition against the Church, but his concession unfortunately obscured many of the instances of the Old Testament which quite vividly support the Church's claims about Jesus. The differences between the supposedly original, but in fact later edited, Hebrew Old Testament and the actually older Greek Septuagint version also fuelled the unhappy division of the Reformation. The older form, backed up by twentieth century findings in the scrolls of Qumran, gives much greater weight to the ancient claims of the Catholic Church.

Even so, in the Western Church at least, we can say that until the sixteenth century, the canon of Scripture was not firmly fixed: there was no one agreed "Bible."

Nor is it a coincidence that the idea of the Bible as a fixed, united text arises at the same time at the printing press. Until then, the Scriptures were transmitted by handwriting, one by one, according to the editorial decisions of the copyist. The idea that the Scriptures are something that most people could own as an object, "my bible," is really quite a new one.

Ownership of a bible would have been a completely alien idea to Jesus and his followers. It should be obvious by now that Jesus could not and did not have a bible of any sort. What he had access to was not a book, but the sacred scrolls of Scripture used in Jewish worship, taken out mostly to be read in their liturgical context.

We should note that for most of Jesus' contemporary Jews, who had lived for centuries under Greek and then Roman rule, they would understand the scriptures only in the Greek version, not the Hebrew. Many (though not all) contemporary Jews spoke Aramaic, and very few could read or understand the ancient Hebrew, so the texts were read from the Greek Septuagint.

We know that the Jewish early Christians were using the Septuagint not least because almost all the quotations of the Old Testament found in the New Testament are taken from it, not from the Hebrew Bible, which has subtle differences even in passages of the 24 books that are in both the Hebrew and Greek texts. Those differences arise, as Margaret Barker has argued, from rabbis editing the texts in the early Christian era so that they did not bolster Christian interpretations.

There is nothing to suggest that Jesus or his contemporaries regarded the 'Apocryphal' Greek texts of the Septuagint as any less authoritative than the Hebrew-only ones: in fact, it was only around AD 90 that Jewish authorities militated towards the Hebrew Scriptures and away from the additional Greek ones — on the grounds that these texts were proving so successful in converting people to Christianity.

Every time we hear someone begin a sentence "the Bible says," these considerations should give us pause. A Christian may rightly believe that the Bible is divinely inspired, written by the Church under the influence of the Spirit, but this should encourage us to take the history of its composition all the more seriously.

Might a Christian not think that God intended for it to be as it is, with all its contradictions and rival voices, its various versions, its fluidity? Had he wished to give us an authoritative, fixed text with one clear and uncontroversial meaning, he could have done so. Indeed, Muslims believe that he has: in the Qur'an.

Likewise, as Muslims are taught he did, Jesus could have written down for us God's message, word for word. The historical evidence suggests that he did not. What he did do, though, is show us how he related, as God's living Word, to the words of the old Scriptures, and there is much we can learn from that relationship.

Throughout the Gospels, Jesus' enemies are always trying to catch him out with scriptural arguments and proof texts, much like the modern fundamentalist. Fortunately, Jesus is well prepared to reply to them. His first recorded bout of verbal sparring must have been good practice. After all, he was out in the wilderness with one of the most well-versed experts in Scripture of all: the Devil.

If this were a Hollywood film, I suppose that the temptations in the wilderness might be presented as a montage of Jesus and the Devil arguing back and forth with a suitably epic soundtrack, for this is Jesus' training for the greater trials that await him, and for spats which will ultimately get him killed.

Roman gladiators were encouraged to train in overweighted armour so that when the real fight came, they would be all the more nimble. Well, Jesus' sparring partner in the desert was a formidable opponent, offering tough practice. Matthew portrays their battle as a rabbinical dialogue, the sort of legal dispute that might go on between learned Pharisees and Sadducees, for example. And to be sure, the Devil knows his Scripture as well as any "Bible teacher."

You can find the first test the Devil puts to Jesus in Matthew 4:3:

> "If you are the Son of God, command these stones to become loaves of bread."

Now, the Devil's first test is not a directly quote from Scripture, but note that each of the Devil's temptations begin with the taunt, "if you are the Son of God" - which *is* a reference to Scripture. Compare Wisdom 2:18:

> "If the righteous man is God's son, he will help him, and will deliver him from the hand of his adversaries."

This taunt sets the tone, as it were, for all three of the temptations. But this first one specifically refers to the sort of thing that the Son of God, or indeed the Messiah, might be expected to do. "Why can't you just turn stones into bread?"

And isn't this just the sort of question that people still ask today about God: if there is a God, then why does he not magic up some food for the millions of starving people all over the world? It sounds like a reasonable request, because there are certainly sentences in Scripture to suggest that God will indeed feed the hungry. If we were to take them literally, as the Devil is doing, we would surely have to wonder why God has not acted on his promises sooner.

The Devil has only half the truth, but even half is enough to make his deceit convincing. Jesus replies by quoting another passage of scripture:

> "It is written, 'Man shall not live by bread alone, but by every word that proceeds from the mouth of God.'"

And indeed, we find that the Devil's demand for Jesus to feed the world as God has promised *is* fulfilled— but not on the Devil's terms. Jesus offers *spiritual* nourishment for the entire world which will give those who seek it eternal life. He foreshadows it in the feeding miracles, and most profoundly in the Last Supper, but realises it on the Cross as he becomes the grain of wheat that produces much fruit, the eternally multiplied bread of life for the whole world, the sacrificial bread that saves from sin and death.

This is not to say that God has not provided enough physical nourishment for the world, either: but it is hardly God's fault that we humans are so bad at sharing what he has given us. This is something we could achieve without miracles. The miracle of forgiveness from sin and eternal life is something far greater, and which we cannot for ourselves achieve at all.

In the second temptation, on top of the Temple in Jerusalem, the Devil cites Scripture with greater precision:

> "If you are the Son of God, throw yourself down; for it is written, 'He will give his angels charge of you,' and 'On their hands they will bear you up, lest you strike your foot against a stone.'" (Matthew 4:6)

Appropriately to the Temple locale, those words are taken directly from one of Psalms sung there in Jewish worship, as they are in Christian worship today (Psalm 91.11 and following). And in fact, Jesus *will* indeed "throw himself down" — into deeper depths than the Devil intends — when he descends into Hell to liberate the dead on Holy Saturday; and he *will* "be borne up" by the angels — higher than the Devil can imagine — at his glorious Ascension, when Christ the divine Word returns to the Father. But he will do this on his Father's terms and at his Father's command, not at the Devil's, directly opposing the Devil's own motive, which is to make Jesus join him in rebellion against the Father.

Again, the Devil takes a single proof text and uses it to tell a one-sided half-truth which sounds so very reasonable. Jesus responds like a true rabbi, with a contradictory text:

"It is written, 'You shall not tempt the Lord your God.'" (Matthew 4:7)

Finally, taking him to a mountain top, the Devil offers Jesus the whole world – at a bargain price:

"All these I will give you, if you will fall down and worship me." (Matthew 4:9)

The Devil's promise may seem unlikely, but certain scriptures, such as 2 Corinthians 4.4 or Ephesians 2.2 do indeed refer to Satan as the god of this world. John's writings also refer to the Prince of this World. So it might reasonably seem that the world is within the Devil's possession to offer to Jesus. Imagine what a wonderful world it would be, if only Jesus had accepted!

But again, Jesus knows that the Devil's principality is only a half-truth. For Jesus, the world is not enough. It is only half of his Kingdom, and (if you will excuse the mathematical contradiction) the lesser half at that. He must be in charge not just of earth, *but of heaven too*, and this gift can be given only by the Father: as indeed it will be, by the time Jesus appears to the disciples on the mountain where he will ascend into heaven after the Resurrection:

> "All authority in heaven and earth has been given to me." (Matthew 28.16)

The Devil can offer only the world as an end in itself. But for Jesus, the world is as nothing unless it is ruled by God's authority, just a shadow of its full potential reality. His Kingdom is ultimately not of this world, and obedience to the Father must come first. So, Jesus again responds with a contradictory text:

> "Begone, Satan! for it is written, 'You shall worship the Lord your God and him only shall you serve.'" (Matthew 4:10)

No doubt, bread and power are important. This world is important. And so, many of Jesus' disciples — most notably among them Peter and Judas — wanted and expected him to take power and feed his people by overthrowing the Romans.

There is much in the Church today, especially in the Liberation Theology movement, that militates towards us humans solving the world's practical ills and imbalances — which is quite right and proper as far as it goes. We cannot love Christ in the tabernacle if we do not love him in the faces of the poor. It becomes problematic when it occludes our ultimate purpose and our ultimate allegiance, though, which is *not* to this world, but to the Kingdom of Heaven.

The results of mere humans trying to forge utopias by our own efforts have been disastrous, as the Thousand Year Reich, the cults of the Dear Leader and the various People's Soviets bear ample witness. The love of God must come first:

> "Except the Lord build the house, they labour in vain that build it." (Psalm 127.1)

So what, in the end, does the Devil have to say about Jesus, the Church and the Bible?

First, I think we have to see that as far as Jesus is concerned, no isolated text of Scripture can be taken alone as the "word of God." When the Devil uses Scripture, *it is not the word of God at all*, any more than "God is great" is the word of God when it is being shouted by a crusader with a Moor's head at his feet. Nor, for that matter, is Scripture the word of God when it is being abused by the Pharisees: to stop Jesus from healing on the Sabbath, for example. Rather, Scripture becomes the word of God only when life is breathed into it by the living Word of God who is Jesus Christ; when it is read with his Spirit, as though with his eyes and voice.

Second, Jesus ultimately does *fulfil* all three of the Devil's temptations, but not in their literal or worldly sense. He fulfils them *spiritually*, through his Cross and Passion, Resurrection and Ascension respectively. It is through the Cross that Jesus becomes the bread which will feed the spiritual hunger of the world. He does this by throwing himself down to the depths and being raised by angels to glory, first to Resurrection in this world, and then through Ascension to heaven. Thus he becomes Lord of both this world and also of the heavens, so that, returning to the words of that ancient Christological hymn, at his name "every knee on earth and in heaven will bend" (Philippians 2.5-11). I would go so far as to say that Jesus' responses to the Devil's wiles are barely comprehensible unless you already have some comprehension of the saving merits of the Cross.

So, this takes us back to where we began: to the testimony of the earliest Christians. It is within the context of *their experience* that their texts make sense, which is to say, *the Bible can be read properly only in the context of the Church which produced it.* But more fundamentally, it is the nature of those early Christians' experience which made them the Church in the first place: that is, their experience of the incarnate, crucified, risen and glorified Christ.

Jesus comes first, the Church comes from Jesus and the Scriptures come from the Church as their written testimony about him. But what are the Scriptures for?

7. THE EUCHARISTIC JESUS

Ask Catholics what keeps their faith going, and most will say, "the Mass."

Ask Protestants the same question, and most will say, "the Bible."

In either case, they may only be saying this because they think it is the proper answer – the real reasons are likely to be more complicated – but even so, this divergence between the Catholic Church and the communities of the Reformation marks a considerable difference in their approach to God.

My own answer would be that both the Mass and the Bible sustain my faith— but I would give firm priority to the Mass. Now, please do not get the impression that this is just a matter of taste, as though ultimately it makes no difference whether one prefers studying the Bible or participating in the sacrifice of Christ and receiving the merits thereof. I am not suggesting at all that they are 'paths up the same mountain.' And to be clear, this is absolutely not just a case of one's preferred 'worship style'— a recent and prevalent notion, which in its divorce of form from content at least verges on heresy. There are solid, historical reasons for Christians to put the Eucharist first.

As we have already seen the early Christians had the Eucharist long before they had what we now know as the Bible. But we can go further than that. In fact, it is reasonable to say that *the Eucharist is the very reason for the formation of the Bible in the first place.* In a nutshell, the Scriptures were collated precisely for reading at the weekly act of Christian worship which was, invariably, the Eucharist.

This is because the Eucharist is the means which Jesus himself gave his followers to participate in and continue the memorial of his Sacrifice on the Cross – the event which gives meaning not just to the Church, but to the entirety of creation.

Even with the advent of Playstations and XBoxes, I believe that primary school children still from time to time enjoy the lo-tech pastime of "Chinese whispers." Sitting in a circle, one child whispers a message to the next, and that child whispers what she thinks she has heard to the next, and so on, until the message comes full circle, generally bearing only a fleeting resemblance to the original.

The essence of much criticism from secularists is that the Church has been playing a two-thousand year game of Chinese whispers with the original message Jesus gave. After all, you need only two or three Christians gathered together to start telling everybody else that they have heard that message wrong. Take the Jehovah's Witnesses, who have recently been mounting an intensive campaign, pushing leaflets through people's doors to tell everyone just how wrong the Church is to place "tradition" above the pure doctrine of the Bible, as they read it. They may well be very pleasant people, but it does bother me that they go to the homes of orthodox Christians and try to pull the wool over their eyes with a little gloss of learning. It leaves people wondering, and sometimes I get people coming to me to ask who has really got Jesus' original message: whom, among so many conflicting voices, they can trust.

I could answer that question by a simple appeal to authority, pointing out that you would be hard-pressed to find a single Jehovah's Witness academic in the theological department of any university in this country, and whilst it would not be the kindest approach, it would not be the worst answer: there is surely some wisdom in trusting the judgement of a tenured scholar over that of an albeit polite and well-meaning couple who come knocking on your door. And indeed, with the caveat that my own conclusions may be wrong, I can only urge interested readers of this little book to pursue more academic tomes on the subject at their leisure. There are many scholars far more authoritative than I.

But it seems to me we have a duty as Christians to defend our faith not just by appeals to authority, but by treating criticism with a respectful and reasoned response; and Catholic Christians certainly do have reasonable things to say about Jesus' original message, and also about those to whom he chose to entrust it.

Two Commandments

Let us think back to the Last Supper. Knowing that this was the night before he would die, Our Lord chose to give two clear commandments to the gathered Apostles. One word in Latin for command is *mandatum*, which is why we give the old English name *Maundy* Thursday to that last day before Good Friday.

You would think, in the circumstances, that these two Maundy Thursday commandments would be important ones, given that they would be Jesus' last private words with the inner sanctum of his disciples before he passed into a new kind of existence. And so they were.

On the night before he died, Our Lord commanded his Apostles:

(1) to break bread and pour wine "in remembrance of him," and

(2) to "love one another" as he had loved them.

And that is it.

What Jesus did *not* command his followers on the night before he died was to go home and read their bibles – which at this stage, did not exist anyway – or to engage in systematic study of Scripture.

This is not to say that the study of the Bible is anything short of praiseworthy: indeed, in the post-Reformation age of ecclesiastical fissiparity and the bargain-basement supermarket of pick-your-own internet-assembled philosophies of the modern secular age, the onus on the Catholic faithful is greater than ever to be well-versed in Holy Writ. We must study our Scriptures, and if we do so will be nourished through them by God the Word, who is Jesus Christ. And what is more, our prayer lives will be greatly enriched by the disciplined practice of Lectio Divina and through the daily recitation of the Divine Office.

But!— no amount of Bible study, or even of prayerful meditation upon its riches, can take the place of Christ himself, as he gives himself to us in the Mass.

Our Lord said "do this in remembrance of me," not "read this in remembrance of me."

Jesus did not whisper his last message before he went to the Cross to an individual, for it to be whispered and distorted down the centuries to come. He did not stick it in a bottle (or a bible) and leave it floating at sea for any random person to pick up and read as they pleased. Instead, he very deliberately *entrusted* his message to his twelve closest followers.

At its most basic level, the "tradition" of the Church simply means the Apostles doing what they were told and passing it on to future generations. And what he told them to do was to worship, in a very specific form, using bread and wine in what we will see was a deliberately ritual meal. Only later did the Church commit Jesus' words and teachings to writing, and only as a means of supplementing that tradition of worship which Jesus himself established.

In the Chinese whispers of many modern Christians, the importance of this meal has been garbled away into insignificance. There are those who hardly see the point in it at all, who see it at best as a "reminder" of what Jesus did for them, but a bare memorial is not what Jesus, or any Jew, would think he was doing as he started the Passover celebrations that night.

To hear some modern sermons about Holy Communion, you would be mistaken for thinking that the Last Supper was Jesus having a casual pub lunch with his mates. Brant Pitre's excellent book, *Jesus and the Jewish Roots of the Eucharist*, shows that the Last Supper, was on the contrary, very much a *ritual* meal. Jesus was deliberately connecting the Jewish ritual of the Old Covenant with the New Covenant which he would complete the next day on the Cross, as the Passover Lamb of God and as the Bread of Life.

The Passover, back in the Old Testament book of Exodus, was the sacrifice of a lamb, its blood daubed on the doorposts of the Jewish people to make the Angel of Death "pass over" their homes and so free them from slavery in Egypt. It is the foundational Jewish story, representing their people's liberation and foreshadowing the ultimate liberation from sin and death promised by God.

In the New Covenant or Testament, Christians believe that Jesus becomes the Lamb of God whose Precious Blood achieves that promise. At the Last Supper, he begins the ritual of the Passover, but does not complete it, refusing to drink the wine: the ritual will be complete only when he is hanging on the Cross. By his sacrifice, Jesus frees not only his own Jewish people, but *all* peoples from the death that sin brings, and so offers everyone eternal life.

Looking at Jesus' own Jewish roots, Pitre makes the vital point that in Jewish eyes, *without the ritual of the Last Supper Jesus' death would not have been a sacrifice at all*. Rather, the Last Supper was the liturgical start-point for the culmination of his sacrifice on the Cross.

So it is that in Church tradition, Maundy Thursday becomes the liturgy which makes Good Friday. By Canon Law, the Mass may not be celebrated on Good Friday, and we instead receive the pre-consecrated host from the Maundy Thursday celebration of the night before. Looking at the historical background, we can see that this is not just some made up bit of Church legalism: rather, it is a sound theological exposition of the historical circumstances of Jesus' self-sacrifice. The Cross would have been no sacrifice were it not for the ritual meal the night before, and so Good Friday is no sacrifice without the celebration of the Eucharist on Maundy Thursday. Our tradition is simply the Church continuing, without deviation, to do as Jesus commanded.

If you are tired of your priest impressing on you every year just how important it is to take part in as much of the Sacred Triduum as you can, perhaps now you can see why.

And yet many still cannot. Many cannot really see the point of the Eucharist at all. Regrettably, I have heard the Eucharist being dismissed as a "barrier to mission," on the grounds that people walking in from the street, unbaptized and unprepared, are not allowed to receive the sacrament (note that they do not make the same complaint about the sacrament of matrimony). I have heard of clergy "consecrating" jelly babies along with the Host so that they have something to give the children. Others have suggested that as a matter of inculturation, in certain parts of the world or among certain demographic groups, we might dispense with bread and wine and consecrate coconuts, or rice and sake, or even a burger and a can of cola instead. The Church, they say, is being stubborn and legalistic in refusing to give the Sacrament to all and sundry, and being culturally insensitive or elitist in limiting it to the staple foods of the West.

So why did Jesus choose to celebrate his final, ritual meal with bread and wine, and why only with his closest followers? Why did he not let all the world in for a late night kebab?

It is not by chance that Jesus chose bread to celebrate that liturgy. Nor was it just because that was his generation's staple food.

The Johannine tradition places particular emphasis on Jesus' claim to be "the Bread of Life," especially in John 5-6. But his connection to this food comes far earlier than that, foreshadowed even in the narratives about his birth in Matthew and Luke. The very name of the village he was born in, Bethlehem, means in Hebrew nothing other than "House of Bread." The first of his temptations in the wilderness was to turn stones into bread. And of course, later in the synoptic gospels, there are the miraculous feedings, in each of which he used loaves of bread. Not least, in the one and only prayer he taught his disciples, there is the reference to what we now translate as our "daily bread"— though the original Greek word, *epiousios*, is a unique word which could well mean 'supernatural' rather than just 'everyday.'

So, long before the Last Supper, bread is a key symbol in Jesus' teaching. We will see just how key it is when we consider its impact in his wider life and ministry.

What's so controversial about bread?

Little is known of Jesus for the first thirty years of his life, during which it is assumed that he worked in his adoptive father's carpentry shop. The stories of his childhood in   Luke speak much more of his mother, Mary, chief of Christian saints— after all, God the Father had chosen her to raise the child who, the angel Gabriel announced to her in a vision, was none other than his only Son.

Around the age of thirty, Jesus spent his forty days of prayer and testing in the wilderness. He was then baptized in the river Jordan by John, the leader of an ascetic Jewish sect who proclaimed Jesus what the Jews call in Hebrew the *Messiah*, meaning 'anointed one:' or, in Greek, the *Christ*. The Jewish scriptures had prophesied the coming of this Messiah and the people had been waiting for generations. Some understood the scriptures promising a king like their ancient King David who would overthrow the Roman occupiers of their land. Not all, though: other Jewish groups expected a spiritual leader who would liberate them from the slavery of sin.

After his baptism, Jesus began preaching and recruiting. He went around the synagogues, places where the many Jews who lived far from the temple in Jerusalem gathered to pray. He already had the recommendation of John the Baptist to build on, and it seems that his message attracted tradesmen of modest education — mostly fishermen at first — and, somewhat controversially, women, too. Unlike other teachers at the time, who sought influence with rich and powerful patrons, he spent his time far away from the southern capital of Jerusalem up in the unfashionable North where people spoke funny, consorting with outcasts: prostitutes, lepers and the hated tax-collectors who were stooges of the Roman regime.

Jesus' teaching was even more controversial than his company. He taught that the rule of God would and should overtake the rule of earthly kings and emperors, calling this the "Kingdom of Heaven." Through repentance, turning back towards God and away from sin, and through baptism, even provincial nobodies could enjoy the Messianic Kingdom he proclaimed.

This did not go down well with the Romans.

His fellow Jews applauded him at first, taking this as a further sign of his messianic status: surely he was the man who would overthrow the oppressor.

But little by little, he provoked his own people, too, both by words and actions. He preached against the hypocrisy of the religious leaders of his day. And far worse than that, he broke their Law: and even worse still, as we saw in Chapter 4, he seemed to place himself above it.

As we saw, for Jews the Law was not some man-made legislation, but God's own Law, or "Torah," revealed hundreds of years before to Moses. So when Jesus started performing miraculous healings on the sacred Sabbath day, when he started calling God "our Father" and taught that children should fight the injustice of their biological parents, when he said that following the letter of the law would get you nowhere with God unless the fundamental law of love was written in your heart, he caused trouble— for himself and for everyone who followed him.

It got worse. Sometimes people prostrated – that is, fell down on their faces – before him, which is worship that Jews should give *only to God*. According to John's gospel, he kept using the Divine Name of "I Am," that unspeakably holy Name YHWH which God had spoken to Moses from the fire of a burning bush, *about himself*. He said *he* would judge the world at the end of time, which was something only God could do. For mainstream Jews, strict monotheists, believers in only one God, this was blasphemy. As I argued in Chapter 4, Jesus seemed to be putting himself in God's place.

But it was when he started telling his followers that they had to *eat his flesh and drink his blood* that they really started deserting him.

At first, they thought he must just be speaking figuratively, using a metaphor, and only a few walked away. But John 5-6 records how he kept pushing the point home, again and again, until only the faithful few remained. When he is questioned about this strange teaching, he even goes to the extent of using a strange word, according to the Greek of St John's Gospel: not only do you have to eat my body, he says, but you have to *trogein* it. *Trogein* means something like "chew," or "gnaw," a very visceral image. Yes, he says, you really do have to chew on my body. It's not just a metaphor. At this point, John tells us, many of the faithful walked away. Cannibalism was just not kosher.

So, Jesus calling himself the Bread of Life and using bread at the Last Supper is not just incidental to his life and teaching. He is not just a mortal rabbi using a very extreme metaphor to make a point. Jesus' talk about bread contributed significantly to his fate of execution on the Cross. His Kingdom talk had made enemies of the Roman rulers, and now his bread talk riled the Jewish religious leaders who appeased them.

Jesus had taught for only three years before his Passion and Crucifixion. His march in roughly AD 33 on Jerusalem, the home of the Jewish temple, defied any expectations of a warrior king. On the day we now mark as Palm Sunday, a week before Easter Day, he approached the city not on a warhorse with armies, but on a foal. The people laid down palm leaves before him, ancient symbols of Jewish rebellion, and shouted slogans comparing him to King David.

Yet, in a few days, when the expected insurrection failed to take place, they would be the same people shouting for his crucifixion.

You see, instead of overthrowing the Romans, it seemed that Jesus wanted to overthrow the Jewish Temple. One of the first things he did on entering Jerusalem was to go into its forecourts, angrily overthrow the tables where animals were being sold for sacrifice, and prophesy that that Temple would fall. And this, too, has much to do with bread.

To understand this, we need to right back to the origin story of the Jewish people, written mostly in the Book of Exodus.

I have mentioned already how Jesus was identified by John with the sacrificial lamb whose blood kept the angel of death from the ancient Israelites' doors as they prepared to flee from the Egyptians. Continuing that ancient story, Moses led his people through the wilderness to Canaan. Exodus 16 tells of how they ran out of food and started grumbling. In answer to Moses' prayer, God provided a strange, flaky, white, bread-like substance. When the Israelites saw it, they said in Hebrew, *man hu?* — "what is it?" — from which we get the English word "Manna." This Manna bread sustained them all the way to Canaan, and mysteriously vanished once they arrived.

And yet in John 6, Jesus had talked about himself as even greater than this angelic manna-bread. That bread only led the Jewish people to the Promised Land of Canaan, and then withered. Those who ate it ultimately died.

In contrast, the new Bread of Jesus' flesh, he said, would last forever and lead to an eternal Kingdom. Those who ate it would live forever.

Jesus was claiming to offer the Jews more than their founding father, Moses, ever could: and, he said, that gift was his very self. This did not endear him to the religious authorities.

Notably, God instructed Moses to keep some of the Manna in the Ark or Tabernacle they carried with them, as a sign of his presence with them— just as in western Catholic tradition, we reserve a portion of the Blessed Sacrament in the Tabernacle or Aumbry as a sign of Christ's presence with us. This aspect of Church tradition, far from being "made up," stretches all the way back to Moses.

More than that, though, the offering and reservation of bread as a sign of God's presence was an essential part of Jewish worship in the Temple even during Jesus' lifetime.

In Leviticus, God had instructed Moses to make twelve stands in the Tabernacle for twelve loaves of bread, one for each of the tribes of Israel. It was called the "Bread of the Presence," supposed to reflect here on earth the eternal bread of God's own presence which Moses saw in the Temple of Heaven. Right up to Jesus' day, every Sabbath, the Jewish priests would bring the sacred bread out before the people and show it to them, this sign of God's presence.

If you are a regular churchgoer, you may be surprised at the words the ancient Jewish priests proclaimed when they elevated this bread: "Behold, the love of God for you!"

Does this sound familiar? If not, look at a missal or pewsheet, and see what the priest says as he elevates the bread over the chalice just after the Agnus Dei: "Behold, the lamb of God…"

Let's put all this symbolism together. There were twelve loaves for twelve tribes in the Temple, and at the Last Supper Jesus broke bread with the twelve Apostles. He entrusted the ritual to them as priests of the New Covenant, saying that this bread would be the sign of God's love for them. Through the sacrifice Jesus was beginning that night in the ritual meal, he was offering the bread of God's loving presence forever, and so making sense of his previous teaching that the bread was none other than his own Body.

And so it is very much in the sacrificial offering of bread that the two Maundy Thursday commandments are linked: "Love one another as I have loved you," and "do this in memory of me."

At the institution of the Mass, Jesus was consecrating himself as the new Lamb of God, replacing the lambs sacrificed every year in the Temple; he was making himself the new Bread of the Presence by which God's love was proclaimed annually from the Temple doors. And so when his prophecy that the Temple would fall came true, in AD 70, it was entirely consistent with everything Jesus had taught and done for the Church to consider itself the continuation of that ancient Temple ritual, but now in a new and bloodless sacrifice, not only for the Jews, but for gentiles too.

Remember that his followers were still hoping that Jesus would lead an armed revolt. This is probably why Judas, who had been a member of a revolutionary outfit called the zealots, lost his patience at this point. Perhaps he saw that it was simply not going to happen. So, he left the feast.

After the meal, Jesus and his disciples retired to a garden called Gethsemane on the Mount of Olives to pray and to sleep. There, Judas brings Roman and Jewish officials to capture Jesus, betraying him with a kiss, which is still a common greeting between men in many Middle Eastern countries today.

Peter, one of Jesus' closest friends, defends him with his sword, wounding a soldier's servant, but Jesus orders him to sheathe it. His warning that those who live by the sword will die by the sword shows a pacifistic instinct which Christians have often not managed to live up to through the ages. Instead of starting an armed revolution, Jesus voluntarily offers himself to die.

So, to the morning of Good Friday. Why "good?" Because it shows how God can turn something designed for evil, for painful torture and death, into the ultimate good, the source of eternal life.

This is the day that Jesus is put on trial by the Roman governor and, at the instigation of his own Jewish people, executed by crucifixion. Consequently Catholic Christians wear crosses, make the sign of the Cross over our bodies during prayer, venerate the Cross by kissing it on Good Friday, abstain from eating meat every Friday, and meditatively pray through the "Stations of the Cross" on church walls, depicting Jesus' final hours. Partly this is out of respect and veneration for a real man who died a real death on a real instrument of torture, but for Christians, it is also much more than that: it is the sign of the real promise of eternal life. If Jesus had just been a wandering rabbi, all we would have left on Good Friday would be a wandering rabbi — and a blasphemous, lying one at that, since he had clearly put himself in the place of God.

Perhaps that is what was going through the disciples' minds, because they all deserted him — most famously Peter, who denied him three times, saying he had nothing to do with this failed revolutionary. Only his mother, Mary, stayed with him at the Cross. His adoptive father, Joseph, was presumably long dead, but another man called Joseph from a place called Arimathea was charged with entombing his body.

It was a popular practice in certain Jewish sects to take parts of martyrs' bodies as relics to inspire zeal and devotion, which may be why the Romans posted guards at the tomb. And yet, according to the scriptures, some time in the night of what we now call Holy Saturday, the stone portal of the tomb was rolled away, and Jesus' follower Mary Magdalene arrived at dawn to find nothing but the grave clothes there. A stranger there spoke to her, and somehow knew her name.

Some intuition told Mary Magdalene that this man was in fact Jesus. It is written that she ran straight to the eleven remaining chief disciples to tell them, so earning herself that title "Apostle to the Apostles," for those eleven were the ones Jesus "sent out" (from the Greek word *apostello*).

Jesus' resurrection is therefore supposed to have happened at some point during the night. This is why Christians have traditionally started celebrating Easter Sunday before dawn, or even during the Saturday night. It also reflects the Jewish tradition that days start not when the sun rises, but when it sets. So it is thanks both to the Resurrection and to Jewish tradition that all Sundays and all of the greater Christian feast days actually begin the evening before, with First Vespers and often a Vigil Mass, too: including the midnight mass on Christmas Eve. This is why Catholics may fulfil their Sunday obligation to attend Mass by attending on Saturday night instead. It is a tradition based not on some whim of the Church for the sake of convenience but on the resurrection of Christ.

The Resurrected Jesus

Our consideration of Sunday eucharistic worship does raise the question as to whether or not Jesus actually rose from the dead. Was this something the Church has made up to exercise power over the minds of the gullible faithful?

The biblical account does not initially look very promising. Jesus is said to have appeared at various times and places to the disciples. In some cases, he showed signs of a physical body: for example, eating with them. In others, he appeared and disappeared almost like a ghost. The disciples did not recognise him until he gave them some sign, generally linked to his breaking of bread at the Last Supper. These mixed biblical accounts suggest quite a confused experience.

What is not confused at all, however, is that the Apostles and several other followers believed very strongly that they had indeed seen the risen Christ. So strongly, in fact, that many would die gruesome deaths rather than deny what they had seen.

There can be no *proof* of the Resurrection, because an empty tomb proves nothing— but the blood of the early martyrs, including St Peter himself, gives plenty of *evidence* for the resurrection, or at least of the strength of the eye-witnesses' belief in what they had seen. Had they simply wanted to peddle the promise of eternal life, as I have mentioned before, there was any number of pagan mystery cults they might have joined without fear of persecution. Yet they chose to die rather than to recant. To me, this suggests that they very firmly believed what they had seen. It is theoretically possible that they were mistaken, but you would have to be very convinced to choose to be thrown to the lions rather than admit a margin of error.

Again, don't let detractors make ammunition from the apparent confusion of the resurrection accounts in the Bible. This just goes to show that the Bible has not been whitewashed by the later Church, as they might like to have you believe. If the Church were so set on brainwashing the masses, why not edit out the mistakes? The fact that the Bible contains different accounts shows a certain integrity and honesty.

But we are jumping ahead of ourselves. Here, we might remind ourselves, that at this stage around AD33, the time of the Resurrection, there was no Bible. There were the scrolls of the Jewish scriptures which Christians now call the "Old Testament," but they were not contained in a single book: they were kept as sacred scrolls to be read and studied in the synagogues, certainly not carried around in any pocket versions.

Jesus did explain those scriptures, but he never held a bible, nor did he ever command his followers to go and read the Bible. Even after the Resurrection, when he explained the Scriptures to the disciples on the Emmaus Road, it was only once he broke bread that they recognised who he was (Luke 24:13-35). His primary command to the Apostles was to take bread and wine as his flesh and blood and celebrate the Eucharist in remembrance of him.

And that is precisely what the Apostles did as they led the earliest Christians in worship: loved one another, and broke bread in remembrance of him.

Jesus' original message, then, was for his Twelve Apostles to make those two commandments the centre of their lives. He entrusted the ritual meal of the Mass especially to those twelve, the final few who had not yet walked away, and before the Bible was even written, they entrusted it to their successors, laying hands on them to start the line of bishops and priests as stewards of that sacred tradition right up to the present day.

So if anyone asks you how to get back beyond the Chinese whispers, back to Jesus' original message, you might tell them to look to the successors of the Apostles: the bishops of the Church which Jesus founded, who gave us our Bible and who, more importantly, continue to offer the Sacrifice Christ entrusted to them of his own body and blood, given once upon the Cross, and for all in the Divine Liturgy of the Eucharist.

POSTSCRIPT: DO UNICORNS EXIST?

■ ■

Presumably, your answer is "no." But it is a question you can answer only because you know what a unicorn would be if it did exist. If you did not, you would not be able to answer. But as it is, you do know that a unicorn, even though it does not exist, is a magical horse with a single horn in its forehead. And knowing that no such horned horses exist, you can answer the question with a fair degree of certainty.

But what if I were to ask you, "do squaggliwumps exist?"

You would not be able to answer without first asking a logically prior question, namely: "what is a squaggliwump?" Unless you know what a squaggliwump is, you can't say whether or not it exists.

If I were then to tell you that a squaggliwump is a rare marsupial found in the lower Andes, you might consider its existence a possibility. Perhaps it does exist, you might think.

If, on the other hand, I were to tell you that a squaggliwump is an intelligent, blue flying rodent from the Milky Way, capable of space travel and telepathic mind control, you would, I hope, conclude that it did not exist. Either way, the question "what is a squaggliwump" must logically precede the question, "do squaggliwumps exist."

So let's get back to the Trinity, and the beginning of this book.

People are very occupied with the question, "does God exist?," and are happy to give firm answers one way or the other. It's a question that can raise hackles easily, for obvious reasons. But it seems to me that people are far too ready to answer this question, whether with a "yes" or a "no," without thinking very much about the logically prior question of *what God actually is*— or, for that matter, is not.

We can easily ask about unicorns' existence because everyone agrees what a unicorn is. We can't easily ask about squaggliwumps' existence, because I just made them up, and nobody knows what they are.

The problem with asking whether God exists is that we all assume that we know and agree what God is. But I think, if you ask even a few Christians what God is, let alone people from other religions and then atheists, you'll get very different answers.

Is God the stern judge? The loving Father? The ruthless dictator? The cruel comedian? The boyfriend substitute? The cause of existence? The absent watchmaker? The energy behind and in all things?

You will find people of all sorts of religions believing in or rejecting variants on all of these "gods."

So is the God that the atheist rejects the same as the God I believe in? Probably not.

Is the God that I believe in the same as the God that Hindus or Muslims or Jews believe in? To be sure, there are some differences. There are even differences between Christians on exactly what God is like. No wonder it is so hard to agree on God's "existence" or otherwise, when we have not even agreed on what God might be. And yet there will certainly be greater conceptual overlap and possibility of fruitful understanding between Christians and Jews or Hindus than with those who are unwilling even to entertain the notion of anything at all beyond the realm of material existence.

I wrote in the introduction that the Trinity is not just a doctrine. Rather, it is the Church's meditation upon that fundamental question of what God is. I do not pretend that it is an easy answer, but then, it is not likely to be. We are, after all, trying to talk about that which is entirely beyond all distinctions of existence and non-existence. We should not be surprised to find thinking about God difficult. But frankly, things that are instantly accessible are seldom worth bothering with. God is worth the effort.

We have made some of that effort in this book. We have tried, with the early Christians, to reconcile the documented evidence that Jesus talked about God as his and our Father, and at the same time talked about himself in terms that could only properly refer to God. The earliest Christians were quite convinced that both the Father and Jesus were God, and that in fact, if you wanted to know what God was, all you had to do was look at Jesus; which is, after all, what Jesus told us himself:

"He who has seen me, has seen the Father." (John 14:9)

The Trinity means that God is like Jesus: or, as Archbishop of Canterbury Michael Ramsey put it, "there is nothing unChristlike in God."

If we can cross the intellectual barrier that prevents us from realising that Jesus and the Father are one, then we are in a position to look at who God really is. All the better if we can guide others across that barrier with us.

We can then start to see God as the Father and the Son, looking at each other for eternity, pouring out their love into Creation through the power of the Holy Spirit.

We can then start to see the Eucharist as the source of that spiritual grace to sustain and redeem us.

We can then start to see the Church, for all her faults, as the apostolic body dedicated to celebrating and guarding this fundamental mystery.

And we can start to see the Bible as a doorway to enter more deeply into the Liturgy, and so into the inner life of Christ in Trinity— who is, all in all, rather more than just a dead, liberal rabbi.

About the Author

Priest, scholar, teacher, Aikido practitioner and lover of all things Japanese, the Rev'd Dr Thomas Plant read Classics at St Andrews University, Scotland, followed by Theology at the universities of Bristol and Cambridge, UK. He currently serves as Chaplain of Lichfield Cathedral School and Visiting Lecturer in Theology at Newman University, Birmingham.

Fr Plant's academic expertise is in Comparative Theology, reflected in his doctoral thesis on Japanese True Pure Land Buddhism and the works of Pseudo-Dionysius.

He has so far eschewed the traditional clerical pastimes of gardening and dog-walking, preferring instead to get thrown around the dojo, to practise his Japanese and to write Lovecraftian horror/sci-fi fiction under the pseudonym of Thomas Idoine.

Printed in Great Britain
by Amazon

36179064R00069